Neuro Linguistic Programming

A User Manual For Your Brain

NLP FOR WEALTH

Unleashing the Power of Your Mind for Prosperity and Abundance

ABHA BHARDWAJ SHARMA

The Miracle Books

INFORMATION

The exercises, techniques, and insights presented in this book are based on the author's own experiences, learnings, and interpretation of information available in the public domain. While they have been carefully curated to assist readers in personal transformation and financial empowerment, individual results may vary.

Readers are encouraged to approach the content with an open mind and to adapt the techniques as they see fit for their personal growth and development.

PREFACE

In the vast expanse of human knowledge, few territories remain as intriguing and as elusive as the realm of our own mind. The interplay of neurons, thoughts, beliefs, and behaviours continues to bewilder and fascinate both experts and laymen alike.

"Neuro-Linguistic Programming: A User Manual For Your Brain" is a bridge that connects two seemingly disparate fields: the intricate sciences of the brain and the art of communication. By converging at the intersection of neuroscience and linguistics, this book serves as a beacon, illuminating the path towards personal and financial empowerment.

As you journey through its pages, you will encounter a harmonious blend of science and strategy, revealing how our very neurons can be allies in our quest for financial prosperity.

Your brain, with its vast networks and powerful capabilities, is the most valuable asset you possess. Yet, many remain unaware of the power that lies dormant within these neural circuits. With the tools and techniques elaborated upon in this book, you are invited to awaken this potential, reprogram the pathways that have held you back, and set forth on a transformative journey towards wealth, abundance, and a deeper understanding of yourself.

A Trilogy

"Unlocking Your Brain's Potential: A User Manual"

Part 1: NLP for Health & Happiness

In the fast-paced modern world, understanding and harnessing the power of your brain is essential for leading a fulfilling life. Welcome to Part 1 of our series, **"NLP for Health & Happiness."** This instalment explores how Neuro-Linguistic Programming (NLP) can be your guide to cultivating optimal well-being and a joyful existence. Through the lens of NLP, we'll delve into techniques that help you rewire your thoughts, communicate effectively, and navigate challenges, all while fostering a lasting sense of happiness and vitality.

Part 2: NLP for Wealth

Embark on a journey to unlock the potential of your brain in the realm of wealth and abundance. **In Part 2 of our series, "NLP for Wealth,"** we explore the fascinating ways NLP can reshape your financial mindset, enhance your decision-making skills, and open doors to opportunities. Discover how your thoughts, beliefs, and language play a pivotal role in attracting prosperity. Whether you're seeking financial freedom, professional success, or a secure future, this part of the series equips you with the tools to manifest wealth with intention and clarity.

Part 3: NLP for Love, Romance & Relationships

Love is a cornerstone of human existence, and your brain plays a central role in shaping the dynamics of your relationships. In Part 3 of our series, **"NLP for Love, Romance & Relationships,"** we delve into the intricacies of human connections. Explore how NLP techniques can enrich your communication, deepen your understanding of emotions, and pave the way for harmonious relationships. Whether you're seeking lasting love, enriching your partnerships, or enhancing your social interactions, this part of the series empowers you to create meaningful and fulfilling bonds.

Join us on this transformative journey as we unlock the intricacies of your brain's potential. From health and happiness to wealth and relationships, NLP becomes your compass, guiding you towards a life of enriched experiences, personal growth, and boundless possibilities.

Part 2

NLP for Wealth

Unleashing the Power of Your Mind for Prosperity and Abundance

Welcome to the captivating second part of our series, "NLP for Wealth." Here, we invite you to embark on a transformative journey into the depths of your mind, where the seeds of prosperity and abundance are sown. In this Part, we delve deeper into the fascinating world of Neuro-Linguistic Programming (NLP) and its profound influence on your financial mindset.

Prepare to explore the extraordinary ways in which NLP can reshape your thoughts, beliefs, and attitudes toward wealth. Discover how it can empower you to make sound financial decisions and uncover hidden opportunities that have the potential to change the course of your financial future. We will shine a light on the pivotal role that your inner dialogues, beliefs, and even the language you use play in attracting and harnessing prosperity.

Whether you're on a quest for financial independence, striving for professional success, or simply looking to build a secure and abundant future, this segment is designed to equip you with the essential tools to manifest wealth with intention, precision, and unwavering clarity. Join us on this enlightening journey as we unravel the transformative power of NLP for wealth, guiding you towards a future adorned with financial abundance and boundless potential. Your wealth journey begins here.

CONTENTS

INTRODUCTION

Neuro-Linguistic Programming (NLP) is a psychological approach and communication model that explores the intricate connection between the neurological processes, language, and patterns of behaviour learned through experience. Developed in the 1970s by Richard Bandler and John Grinder, NLP is founded on the belief that by understanding and manipulating the ways our mind processes information, we can achieve more effective communication, personal development, and behavioural change.

Neuro-Linguistic Programming, or NLP for short, is like a user manual for your brain. Imagine if you could learn the secrets of how your mind works, how you communicate with yourself and others, and how to make positive changes in your life – that's what NLP is all about!

At its heart, NLP is all about understanding how our thoughts, feelings, and actions are connected. It's like uncovering the hidden patterns in our minds that shape the way we see the world and react to it. Just like learning to read a map, NLP helps us navigate through our thoughts and behaviours.

The "neuro" part of NLP refers to our nervous system – our brain and all the signals it sends to our body. Think of it as the hardware of your mind. The "linguistic" part is about the language we use – both the words we say and the way we say them. It's like the software that runs on our mental hardware.

But here's the really cool part: NLP gives us tools to reprogram that software! It's like having a superpower to change the way we think and act.

You can use NLP to conquer fears, build confidence, and even improve your communication with others.

It's a bit like learning the tricks of magicians. NLP helps us understand the tricks our minds play on us, and how we can use those tricks to our advantage. It's not about reading minds, but about understanding how minds read the world.

In everyday life, NLP can be used to break bad habits, boost motivation, and improve relationships. Whether you want to give a killer presentation, overcome a fear of lizards, or simply be more in control of your thoughts and emotions, NLP offers a toolkit to help you do just that.

So, if you're curious about your mind's inner workings and want to learn how to tap into its full potential, NLP might just be the key. It's a fascinating journey into the world of human behavior and communication that can unlock a whole new level of understanding and personal growth.

Wealth generally refers to a plentiful supply of valuable resources, possessions, or assets that have economic value. While the concept of wealth often involves financial and material abundance, it can also encompass a broader range of resources, including knowledge, health, relationships, and personal well-being. Wealth is subjective and can vary based on individual perspectives and cultural contexts. It's not solely about the accumulation of resources, but also about their effective management and the ability to fulfill one's desires and needs.

Money is a widely accepted medium of exchange that holds economic value and is used as a unit of account for goods, services, and transactions. It is a tangible representation of wealth and is essential for conducting economic activities within a society. Money serves several functions, including facilitating trade, measuring value, storing purchasing power over time, and acting as a standard of deferred payment. Different forms of money exist, such as coins, banknotes, digital currency, and electronic transactions. While money is a crucial aspect of financial well-being, it's important to note that wealth encompasses a broader range of resources beyond just monetary assets.

As humans, our needs encompass both wealth and money, but the emphasis on each can vary based on individual circumstances, values, and priorities.

Here's a breakdown of why both aspects are important:

Money:

Money is a practical necessity in our modern society. It's required to fulfill our basic needs, such as food, shelter, clothing, and healthcare. Having enough money ensures that we can provide for ourselves and our families, maintain a certain standard of living, and address immediate financial responsibilities. Money offers a sense of security, especially in emergencies and unexpected situations.

Wealth:

Wealth goes beyond monetary resources and includes a broader range of factors that contribute to overall well-being and quality of life. Building wealth in terms of knowledge, relationships, health, personal growth, and fulfillment adds depth and meaning to our existence. Wealth enables us to lead a life that aligns with our values, aspirations, and passions. It allows us to invest in personal growth, create strong bonds with loved ones, and find purpose in contributing to society.

Balancing Money and Wealth:

While money is essential for meeting basic needs, wealth provides a more holistic and fulfilling life experience. Striking a balance between the two is crucial. Overemphasising money at the expense of other aspects of wealth can lead to a lack of fulfilment, strained relationships, and neglect of personal growth. On the other hand, solely focusing on wealth without considering financial stability can lead to practical difficulties.

Ultimately, the pursuit of wealth should be aimed at enhancing our overall well-being. It's about leveraging financial resources to create opportunities for personal growth, meaningful experiences, and a purposeful life.

Chapter 1 Brain, Neurons, NLP & Wealth

The Marvels of the Human Brain and Neurons

The human brain, an intricate masterpiece of nature, stands as the epicentre of our thoughts, emotions, and actions. Within its complex folds, a remarkable dance of neurons takes place, orchestrating the symphony of our consciousness. Let's embark on a journey to uncover the wonders of the brain and the role of neurons in shaping our perceptions and experiences.

The Brain: A Universe Within

Envision the brain as a universe within, composed of billions of cells called neurons. It's not just an organ; it's a cosmos of connections. This three-pound powerhouse drives our every move, from breathing to creating art. It's where dreams are born, decisions are made, and memories are stored. Divided into distinct regions responsible for diverse functions—thinking, feeling, remembering—each region contributes to the multifaceted nature of human existence.

Neurons: Messengers of Thought

At the heart of this cosmic network are neurons—tiny messengers that transmit electrical and chemical signals. Neurons are the architects of our thoughts, forming complex pathways that light up with activity when we think, learn, or feel. Their structure is reminiscent of a tree, with branches (dendrites) receiving information, a cell body processing it, and an axon transmitting it onward. These intricate connections form neural networks, the building blocks of our thoughts and behaviours.

The Dance of Synapses

The conversation between neurons occurs at synapses, microscopic gaps where chemical messengers (neurotransmitters) jump from one neuron to another. This dance of neurotransmitters facilitates the transmission of information, allowing us to perceive, learn, and respond to the world around us. It's a delicate interplay that influences our moods, decisions, and even the formation of memories.

Neuroplasticity: The Brain's Adaptability

One of the brain's most astonishing traits is its ability to adapt and rewire itself, known as neuroplasticity. Throughout life, new connections form and old ones weaken, sculpting the brain's structure based on experiences, learning, and environmental factors. This malleability is what enables us to recover from injuries, learn new skills, and navigate the complexities of life.

In the grand tapestry of existence, the human brain and its neurons are threads woven intricately. From the tiniest thought to the grandest ambition, these neural symphonies compose the melody of our lives, guiding us through the vast landscape of human experience.

Brain Neurons and NLP: The Pathways to Transformation

Within the vast expanse of the human brain, a profound synergy between neurons and Neuro-Linguistic Programming (NLP) takes center stage. As we dive into the intricate realm of brain activity, we discover how NLP harnesses the power of neural connections to facilitate personal transformation, communication mastery, and the cultivation of a purposeful life.

Neurons as the Catalysts of Change

Neurons, often referred to as the brain's building blocks, are at the heart of every thought, emotion, and action we experience. These microscopic messengers communicate through electrical impulses and chemical signals, creating intricate networks that weave the fabric of our cognition. In the context of NLP, neurons serve as the pathways along which our thoughts, beliefs, and behaviors traverse. NLP techniques leverage these neural pathways to rewire limiting beliefs, replace negative thought patterns, and amplify our innate potential.

NLP: Illuminating the Pathways of Transformation

Neuro-Linguistic Programming, as its name suggests, fuses neuroscience with linguistics to unlock the potential of human communication and cognition. It recognizes that our mental processes are deeply intertwined with our language patterns and behaviors. Through NLP, we gain the ability to consciously reprogram these patterns, leading to a profound shift in our perception of reality. By aligning our internal dialogue, body language, and mental images with our desired outcomes, NLP empowers us to craft a narrative that reflects our aspirations.

Neural Plasticity and NLP's Influence

The brain's remarkable adaptability, known as **neural plasticity,** forms a pivotal bridge between neurons and NLP. This phenomenon allows us to reshape neural connections based on our experiences and intentions. When we engage in NLP practices, we tap into the brain's plasticity to create new pathways that support our personal growth and transformation. Whether it's reframing limiting beliefs, employing visualization techniques, or modeling successful behaviors, NLP harnesses the brain's inherent plasticity to sculpt a more empowered and purposeful existence.

In the synergy between brain neurons and NLP, we uncover a dynamic interplay that holds the key to unlocking our fullest potential. Through NLP's techniques, we navigate the neural landscape with intention, shaping our thoughts, beliefs, and actions to align with our aspirations. As you journey further into the realm of NLP, you'll witness how the convergence of neuroscience and linguistics can catalyze profound transformations, enabling you to rewrite the script of your life with intention and purpose.

Neurons, Money, and NLP: Rewiring for Wealth and Abundance

Within the intricate tapestry of brain neurons lies a profound connection to our perceptions of money and abundance. As we navigate the realms of thought and finance, Neuro-Linguistic Programming (NLP) emerges as a transformative tool, allowing us to reshape our neural pathways and align our mindset with the wealth and abundance we desire.

Neural Pathways: Mapping Our Money Mindset
Neurons, those remarkable messengers of the brain, play a pivotal role in shaping our relationship with money. The neural pathways formed through our experiences, upbringing, and beliefs shape our financial attitudes and behaviors. Whether we harbor limiting beliefs about money or exude a positive abundance mindset, these neural connections have a significant impact on our financial reality. NLP steps in by offering techniques to rewire these pathways, enabling us to replace scarcity-based thinking with thoughts of prosperity.

Money and Abundance through NLP
Enter the realm of NLP, where the synergy between neurology, language, and programming intertwines with our financial aspirations. NLP techniques provide a roadmap to decode the language of our thoughts, altering negative self-talk, and fostering a deep sense of abundance. Visualization exercises align our

subconscious with our financial goals, while reframing techniques reshape our perceptions of wealth. By mastering NLP, we gain the tools to transform our inner dialogue, attitudes, and actions, paving the way for the manifestation of financial success.

Neural Plasticity and Wealth Creation

Neural plasticity, the brain's ability to adapt and rewire itself, serves as the bridge between neurons, money, and NLP. This remarkable feature allows us to reshape our brain's neural connections in response to intentional practices. As we immerse ourselves in NLP techniques, our brain's plasticity enables us to let go of scarcity-based neural pathways and cultivate those that align with prosperity.

By consciously rewiring our neural circuits, we set the stage for a profound shift in our financial consciousness, enabling us to attract wealth and abundance with clarity and intention.

In the convergence of neurons, money, and NLP, we unveil a transformative journey towards financial empowerment. Through NLP's lens, we gain insights into the neural mechanisms that drive our financial attitudes, and we harness the power to rewrite those pathways for prosperity. As you engage in NLP practices, envision the potential to create a new neural narrative—one that embraces abundance, opens doors to opportunities, and guides you toward the realization of your financial aspirations.

Chapter 2 NLP : The Various Techniques

Neuro-Linguistic Programming (NLP) techniques can indeed be used to enhance your mindset and actions towards wealth creation and attraction. NLP focuses on the connection between neurological processes, language, and behavioral patterns. Here are some NLP techniques that can help you align your mindset and actions with wealth creation:

Visualisation: Create vivid mental images of your desired wealth-related goals. Imagine yourself achieving financial success, living a prosperous life, and enjoying the benefits of wealth. Engage all your senses in this visualisation to make it more impactful.

Anchoring Positive Emotions: Use anchoring techniques to associate positive emotions with wealth-related thoughts and actions. Whenever you think about financial success, anchor that positive feeling by touching a specific part of your body, like pressing your thumb and forefinger together.

Positive Affirmations: Craft positive and empowering affirmations related to wealth. Repeat these affirmations daily, preferably in front of a mirror, to reprogram your subconscious mind for abundance. For example, "I am worthy of wealth and success."

Belief Restructuring: Identify and challenge any limiting beliefs you have about money and wealth. Replace them with empowering beliefs that align with your wealth goals. Use techniques like reframing to change the perspective of negative beliefs.

Modeling Success: Study the behaviors, habits, and mindset of successful individuals who have achieved wealth. Model their strategies and adopt their positive thought patterns to create similar success for yourself.

Goal Setting with Precision: Use the SMART (Specific, Measurable, Achievable, Relevant, Time-Bound) goal-setting framework to define clear wealth-related goals. This helps your subconscious mind focus on specific outcomes.

Future Pacing: Mentally project yourself into the future where you have achieved your financial goals. Visualize your daily life, the opportunities you have, and the emotions you experience. This creates a strong motivational pull towards your desired outcome.

Language Patterns: Be mindful of the language you use when talking about money and wealth. Replace negative phrases like "I can't afford it" with positive ones like "I am working towards affording it."

Creating Wealth Rituals: Develop daily rituals that align with wealth creation. This could include reading wealth-related materials, affirmations, visualizations, and taking inspired actions towards your financial goals.

Neurological Repatterning: NLP techniques like submodalities can help you change the way you internally represent wealth-related thoughts. Modify sensory components like images, sounds, and feelings to influence your response to money-related stimuli.

Remember that while NLP techniques can be powerful tools, they should be combined with consistent action, financial education, and a proactive approach towards wealth creation. Additionally, working on your mindset and behaviors takes time, so be patient and persistent in your efforts.

We will learn about each technique in detail

Chapter 3 Visualization

Visualization is a powerful technique used to create a mental picture of your desired goals and outcomes. By engaging your imagination and senses, you can enhance your belief in achieving those goals, which can, in turn, influence your actions and mindset. Here's a detailed guide on how to effectively use visualization for wealth-related goals:

Find a Quiet Space: Choose a quiet and comfortable space where you won't be disturbed. This could be a room, a comfortable chair, or any place where you can relax without distractions.

2. Relax and Breathe: Sit or lie down in a relaxed position. Close your eyes and take a few deep breaths to calm your mind and body

3. Choose a Wealth Goal: Select a specific wealth-related goal that you want to visualize. It could be achieving a certain income level, starting a successful business, or any other financial aspiration.

4. Set the Scene:
Begin by creating a detailed mental image of the scenario where you've achieved your goal.
Imagine the environment around you. Are you in a luxurious home, an office, or a serene outdoor location?
Visualize the details of your surroundings, such as colors, textures, and objects.

5. Engage Your Senses:
To make your visualization more impactful, engage all your senses: sight, sound, touch, smell, and taste.
Visualize how everything looks—the colors, shapes, and details.
Imagine the sounds you would hear in that scenario, like the clinking of glasses in celebration or the sound of success.

Feel the textures around you, whether it's the softness of a luxurious fabric or the cool touch of success.
Imagine any scents in the air, such as the fragrance of accomplishment and abundance.
If relevant, imagine tasting a symbol of your success, like a celebratory meal or a favorite treat.

6. Embrace the Emotion:
While visualizing, evoke the positive emotions associated with achieving your wealth goal. Feel the excitement, joy, and fulfillment as if it's happening in the present moment.

7. Add Movement:
If it feels natural, add movement to your visualization. Imagine yourself confidently taking actions that align with your wealth goal.

8. Stay in the Moment:
Spend a few minutes immersed in this visualization, living out your success in your mind. The longer and more vividly you can visualize, the better.

9. Express Gratitude:
Before you end the visualization, take a moment to express gratitude for the success you've visualized. This adds a positive energy to your visualization.

10. Repeat Regularly:
Practice this visualization regularly—ideally daily—to reinforce your belief in your wealth-related goals and to align your actions and mindset with achieving them.

Visualization works by aligning your subconscious mind with your goals, making them feel more attainable and real. The more detailed and emotionally charged your visualization, the more effective it can be in reshaping your mindset and actions towards wealth creation.

Chapter 4 : Anchoring

Anchoring is a technique derived from Neuro-Linguistic Programming (NLP) that involves associating a specific physical touch, gesture, or action with a particular emotional state. The goal is to create a connection between the anchor and the emotion so that triggering the anchor in the future can help you access that desired emotional state. Here's how you can use anchoring to associate positive emotions with wealth-related thoughts and actions:

Choose a Positive Emotion: Begin by identifying a positive emotion that you want to associate with your wealth-related thoughts and actions. This could be a feeling of confidence, abundance, excitement, or any other emotion that resonates with your financial goals.

2. Create a Unique Anchor: Choose a simple and distinct physical touch or gesture that you can easily replicate whenever you want to activate that positive emotion. For example, pressing your thumb and forefinger together, as you mentioned.

3. Set the Anchor: Find a quiet and comfortable place where you won't be distracted. Close your eyes and take a few deep breaths to relax. Now, vividly recall a moment when you experienced the chosen positive emotion. Imagine that situation as vividly as possible, feeling the emotion in your body.

4. Apply the Anchor: While you're immersed in the positive emotion, apply the chosen physical touch or gesture (e.g., pressing your thumb and forefinger together). Keep experiencing the emotion while you do this.
5. Release and Test: After a few seconds of applying the anchor, release the touch or gesture and let go of the emotion. Open your eyes and distract yourself for a moment to reset your mind.

6. Test the Anchor: Now, press your thumb and forefinger together again, trying to evoke the same positive emotion. Recall the moment when you felt that emotion strongly. Repeat the anchor a few times while recalling the memory to reinforce the association.

7. Practice: Repeat the process several times over the course of a few days. The more you practice, the stronger the association between the anchor and the positive emotion will become.

8. Use the Anchor: In the future, whenever you want to access that positive emotion to align yourself with wealth-related thoughts or actions, simply press your thumb and forefinger together. This anchor can be used before financial decision-making, goal-setting sessions, or whenever you need a boost of positivity related to wealth.

Remember that anchoring works best when you're in a relaxed and receptive state. Consistent practice is key to strengthening the association between the anchor and the desired emotion. Over time, this technique can help you naturally evoke positive feelings related to wealth, creating a more empowered mindset for financial success.

Chapter 5 : Positive Affirmations

Positive affirmations are powerful statements that you repeat to yourself to cultivate a positive and empowered mindset. When it comes to wealth-related affirmations, the goal is to reshape your beliefs about money and abundance, thereby reprogramming your subconscious mind for success. Here's a detailed guide on crafting and using positive affirmations for wealth.

Identify Your Beliefs: Start by recognizing any negative beliefs or thought patterns you may have about money. These might include beliefs like "Money is hard to come by" or "I'll never be wealthy." Identifying these limiting beliefs is the first step toward transforming them.

2. Craft Empowering Affirmations:
Use the present tense: Phrase your affirmations in the present tense as if you already possess the wealth and success you desire.
Be positive: Focus on what you want, not what you want to avoid. Frame your affirmations positively.
Make them personal: Tailor the affirmations to resonate with your goals and aspirations.
Keep them concise: Keep your affirmations short and specific to ensure clarity and impact.

3. Examples of Wealth Affirmations:
"I am a magnet for financial abundance, and wealth flows to me effortlessly."
"I am open to receiving wealth from multiple sources in my life."
"I deserve to be wealthy, and I embrace the opportunities that come my way."
"I am aligned with the energy of abundance, and I attract prosperity into my life."
"I am grateful for the wealth that is constantly flowing into my life."

4. Set a Routine:
Choose a specific time of day, preferably morning or before bedtime, to practice your affirmations.

Stand in front of a mirror, make eye contact with yourself, and speak the affirmations aloud with conviction.

5. Engage Emotions:
As you repeat your affirmations, feel the emotions associated with them. Imagine how it feels to be wealthy and successful.
Visualization can enhance the emotional impact. Imagine yourself living the life you desire.

6. Repetition and Consistency:
Repeat your affirmations daily. Consistency is key to reinforcing positive beliefs in your subconscious mind.
Repetition helps overwrite old negative beliefs with new empowering ones.

7. Believe and Let Go:
As you repeat your affirmations, believe in their truth. Even if you don't fully believe them at the start, the repetition will gradually shift your mindset.
Let go of doubts and skepticism. Trust in the process and your ability to create positive change.

8. Celebrate Progress:
As you begin to notice shifts in your mindset and actions, celebrate your progress. Acknowledge even the smallest positive changes.
Using positive affirmations consistently over time can lead to a transformation in your beliefs about wealth and success.
Remember that while affirmations are a powerful tool, they are most effective when combined with proactive actions, financial education, and a positive attitude toward opportunities.

Wealth affirmations that you can use to cultivate a prosperous and abundant mindset:

"I am a magnet for financial abundance, and prosperity flows to me effortlessly."
"I deserve to be wealthy, and I am open to receiving all the wealth the universe has to offer."
"Every day, in every way, I am becoming wealthier and more financially empowered."
"I am aligned with the energy of abundance, and I attract lucrative opportunities into my life."
"My wealth is a reflection of the value I bring to the world, and I am worthy of immense financial success."
"I am in control of my financial destiny, and I make wise and abundant choices."
"The universe supports my financial goals, and I am grateful for the wealth that flows to me."
"I am releasing any limiting beliefs about money and embracing a mindset of endless prosperity."
"I confidently take inspired actions that lead to wealth creation and financial freedom."
"As my wealth grows, I have the ability to make a positive impact on my life and the lives of others."

Remember to personalize these affirmations to resonate with your goals and aspirations. Repeat them daily with conviction, visualize the outcomes, and let the positive emotions associated with abundance flow through you. With consistent practice, these affirmations can help you transform your relationship with wealth and attract financial success into your life.

Chapter 6 Belief Restructuring

Belief restructuring is a transformative process that involves identifying and challenging any negative or limiting beliefs you hold about money and wealth. By replacing these beliefs with positive and empowering ones, you can reshape your mindset and open yourself up to greater financial abundance. Here's a detailed guide on how to effectively restructure your beliefs:

1. Self-Reflection:
Take some time to reflect on your beliefs about money. Write down any negative beliefs that you notice, such as "Money is the root of all evil" or "I'll never be wealthy."
Pay attention to any patterns or recurring thoughts that hold you back from embracing a positive relationship with wealth.

2. Question Your Beliefs:
Examine the beliefs you've identified and ask yourself if they are based on facts or assumptions.
Consider whether these beliefs have been inherited from others, societal conditioning, or past experiences.

3. Gather Evidence:
Challenge your limiting beliefs by collecting evidence that contradicts them. Look for examples of people who have achieved financial success despite circumstances similar to yours.

4. Reframe Negative Beliefs:
Once you've identified a negative belief, reframe it into a positive statement that aligns with your wealth goals.
For instance, if you believe "Money is the root of all evil," reframe it as "Money is a tool that allows me to make a positive impact on my life and others."
5. Affirmations for Empowerment:

Craft positive affirmations that counteract your old negative beliefs. Repeat these affirmations daily to reinforce your new empowering beliefs.
For example, if you used to believe "I'll never be wealthy," your affirmation could be "I am open to receiving wealth and creating financial abundance."

6. Visualization of Success:
Visualize scenarios where you have successfully overcome your limiting beliefs and achieved financial success.
Imagine yourself confidently making financial decisions and enjoying the benefits of wealth.

7. Seek Support:
Discuss your beliefs with supportive friends, mentors, or coaches who can provide alternative perspectives and encourage your personal growth.

8. Journaling:
Keep a journal where you write down your old limiting beliefs, their reframed versions, and your progress in adopting new empowering beliefs.

9. Consistency and Patience:
Changing beliefs is a process that takes time. Consistently challenge and reframe your negative beliefs as they arise.
Be patient with yourself, and celebrate small victories along the way.

10. Stay Open to Learning:
Be open to learning about money management, investing, and financial literacy. Education can help challenge and change your beliefs.

By restructuring your beliefs and replacing negative thoughts with positive ones, you are creating a mental framework that supports your wealth-related goals. Remember that belief restructuring is an ongoing process, and with dedication, you can transform your mindset to align with your aspirations for financial abundance.

Chapter 7 Reframing Negative Beliefs

Reframing negative beliefs into positive statements involves shifting the perspective of the belief to create a more empowering and constructive thought. Here's a step-by-step process on how to reframe negative beliefs into positive affirmations:

1. Identify the Negative Belief:
Recognize the negative belief you want to reframe. Write it down so you can clearly see the thought that needs transformation.

2. Challenge the Negative Belief:
Question the validity of the negative belief. Ask yourself if it's based on facts, assumptions, past experiences, or external influences.

3. Find the Positive Counterpart:
Consider the opposite perspective or a more balanced view that aligns with your goals and values.
Focus on the constructive aspect of the belief, rather than its limitations.

4. Craft the Positive Reframe:
Transform the negative belief into a positive statement that embodies your desired perspective.
Make it specific, concise, and emotionally resonant.

5. Use Empowering Language:
Use affirmative and empowering language in your reframed statement.
Replace words like "can't" with "can," "won't" with "will," and "never" with “always."

6. Make it Personal:

Tailor the reframed statement to reflect your personal experiences and aspirations.
This makes the affirmation more relatable and meaningful to you.

7. Example
Original Negative Belief: "I'll never have enough money to enjoy life."
Positive Reframe: "I am creating a life of financial abundance that allows me to enjoy all the experiences I desire."

8. Ensure it Feels Authentic
Your reframed statement should resonate with you and feel authentic. It should inspire positive emotions and confidence.

9. Repeat and Reinforce:
Repeat your positive reframed statement regularly, ideally daily. This repetition helps rewire your thought patterns.

10. Visualize the New Perspective:
When using the reframed statement, visualize scenarios where this new perspective is evident in your life.
Feel the emotions associated with this positive belief.

11. Embrace the Change:
Be open to embracing the new perspective and make a conscious effort to replace the old negative belief with the positive one. Remember that the goal of reframing is to shift your mindset and beliefs towards a more constructive and empowering outlook. As you consistently use these reframed statements, you'll find that your thought patterns begin to align with your wealth goals, creating a more conducive environment for financial success

Chapter 8 Modelling Success

Modelling success involves studying the behaviours, habits, and mindset of individuals who have achieved the type of success you aspire to, in this case, financial success and wealth. By learning from their experiences and emulating their strategies, you can increase your chances of achieving similar outcomes. Here's a detailed guide on how to effectively model success:

1. Identify Role Models:
Choose successful individuals who have achieved the level of financial success you desire. They can be entrepreneurs, investors, authors, or anyone who has a track record of wealth creation.

2. Study Their Journey:
Research their life stories, biographies, interviews, and any available materials that provide insights into their path to success. Understand their background, challenges, pivotal moments, and decisions that contributed to their success.

3. Observe Behaviours and Habits:
Pay attention to the behaviours and habits that these successful individuals exhibit. This can include their work ethic, time management, networking, and dedication to self-improvement.

4. Analyse Mindset:
Study their mindset, attitudes, and beliefs about money, wealth, and success.
Identify how they approach challenges, setbacks, and opportunities.

5. Extract Key Strategies:
Identify the specific strategies and tactics that have contributed to their success. These could include investment strategies, business models, decision-making processes, and more.

6. Emulate Positive Thought Patterns:
Adopt the positive thought patterns and beliefs that have helped these successful individuals overcome obstacles and maintain a growth-oriented mindset.

Challenge and replace your own limiting beliefs with the empowering beliefs of these role models.

7. Set Goals and Action Plans:
Define clear financial goals based on the insights you've gained from studying these role models.
Create actionable plans that incorporate the strategies you've learned from their experiences.

8. Implement Gradually:
Start integrating the habits and strategies of your role models into your daily routine. It's important to start small and build consistency over time.

9. Stay Adaptable:
While modelling success, remember that every individual's journey is unique. Adapt the strategies to fit your personal circumstances and goals.

10. Seek Direct Guidance:
If possible, attend seminars, workshops, or conferences where these successful individuals share their insights and experiences. Networking opportunities can provide direct access to their knowledge and expertise.

11. Regularly Review and Adjust:
Continuously assess your progress and refine your approach. Regularly revisit the behaviours, habits, and strategies that you've learned from your role models.

12. Maintain a Growth Mindset:
Approach modelling success as an ongoing process of learning and improvement. Stay open to new ideas and remain dedicated to your personal growth.

Modelling success is about adapting proven strategies while also staying authentic to your own journey. By learning from those who have achieved wealth, you can accelerate your own path to financial success and gain valuable insights that help you navigate challenges more effectively.

Chapter 9 The SMART Goal-Setting Framework

The SMART goal-setting framework is a widely used approach to defining clear and actionable goals. When it comes to wealth-related goals, using the SMART framework can provide structure and clarity, helping you set objectives that are more likely to lead to success. Here's a detailed breakdown of how to apply the SMART criteria to your wealth-related goals:

1. Specific:
Clearly define the specific wealth-related goal you want to achieve. Avoid vague statements and ensure your goal is precise and well-defined.
Instead of a general goal like "I want to be wealthy," make it specific: "I want to increase my monthly income by 20% within the next year."

2. Measurable:
Make your goal measurable by including quantifiable criteria that will help you track your progress and determine when you've achieved the goal.
Instead of saying "I want to save more money," specify: "I want to save $10,000 over the next 12 months."

3. Achievable:
Your goal should be realistic and attainable based on your current resources, skills, and circumstances.
While aiming high is good, ensure that your goal is within reach. For instance, setting a goal to double your income in a month might not be achievable, but doubling it in a year could be more reasonable.

4. Relevant:
Ensure that your wealth-related goal is relevant to your overall aspirations and aligns with your values and long-term objectives. Consider how achieving this goal fits into your larger financial plan and contributes to your overall well-being.

5. Time-Bound:
Set a specific timeframe for achieving your goal. This adds a sense of urgency and accountability to your goal-setting process.

Instead of saying "I want to invest in stocks," make it time-bound: "I want to invest $5,000 in stocks within the next three months.”

Applying SMART to Wealth Goals:

Let's say your wealth-related goal is to pay off your student loans:
Specific: "I want to pay off my $20,000 student loan debt."
Measurable: "I will make extra payments of $1,000 per month towards my student loan."
Achievable: "I will allocate a portion of my monthly income towards the extra payments without compromising my basic needs."
Relevant: "Paying off my student loan will free up funds for other financial goals and reduce my financial stress."
Time-Bound: "I will pay off my $20,000 student loan debt within 18 months."
By using the SMART framework, you create a well-defined and structured goal that guides your actions and provides a clear roadmap for achieving your wealth-related aspirations. This clarity can help your subconscious mind focus on specific outcomes and motivate you to take consistent steps toward your financial success.

Chapter 10 Future Pacing

Future pacing is a technique that involves mentally projecting yourself into the future and experiencing the success you've achieved. This visualisation exercise can be incredibly motivating and help solidify your commitment to your financial goals. Here's a step-by-step guide on how to effectively use future pacing to enhance your motivation and focus on your desired financial outcome:

1. Choose a Timeframe:
Decide on a specific timeframe in the future that you want to envision. It could be a year, five years, or any period that aligns with your financial goals

2. Create a Vivid Picture:
Close your eyes and imagine yourself at that point in the future when you have achieved your financial goals. Visualise the scene with as much detail as possible.

3. Engage Your Senses:
Make the visualisation as real as you can. Engage all your senses: what do you see, hear, feel, smell, and even taste in this successful scenario?

4. Imagine Your Daily Life:
Visualise your daily routine in this successful future. What do you do when you wake up? How do you spend your day? Imagine the activities, interactions, and tasks you're engaged in.

5. Embrace the Emotions:
Feel the emotions associated with your success. Experience the joy, satisfaction, and fulfillment that come from achieving your financial goals.

6. Explore Opportunities:
Envision the opportunities that are available to you now that you've achieved your financial goals. What new ventures, experiences, or adventures can you pursue?

7. Visualize Challenges:
While it's important to focus on the positive, also imagine any challenges that may arise even after achieving your goals. Visualize how you overcome these challenges with resilience and determination.

8. Absorb the Learning:
Consider the lessons you've learned on your journey to financial success. How have these experiences shaped your mindset and approach to wealth?

9. Connect with the Future Self:
Mentally connect with your future self. Feel a sense of gratitude for the steps you've taken to get there.

10. Return to the Present:
Slowly transition back to the present moment. Open your eyes and take a moment to reflect on the visualization experience.

11. Harness the Motivation:
Use the emotions and motivation you've gathered from this exercise to fuel your actions and decisions in the present. Let the positive feelings guide your commitment to your financial goals.

Future pacing helps you align your present actions with your desired future outcomes. By vividly experiencing your success in advance, you create a strong psychological connection to your goals and enhance your determination to make them a reality.

Chapter 11 Language Patterns

Language plays a significant role in shaping our thoughts, beliefs, and actions. When it comes to money and wealth, using positive and empowering language can have a profound impact on your mindset and financial outcomes. Here's a detailed guide on how to be mindful of your language patterns and replace negative phrases with positive ones:

1. Identify Negative Phrases:
Pay attention to the language you use when discussing money, wealth, and financial matters. Notice any negative or disempowering phrases you commonly use.

2. Challenge Negative Language:
Challenge the negative phrases and beliefs you've identified. Ask yourself if they are based on facts or if they're limiting your mindset.

3. Reframe with Positive Language:
Replace negative phrases with positive ones that reflect a growth-oriented and proactive mindset.

4. Examples of Language Patterns:
Negative Phrase: "I can't afford it."
Positive Reframe: "I am working towards affording it. I am taking steps to improve my financial situation."

Negative Phrase: "I'm bad with money."
Positive Reframe: "I am learning to manage my finances effectively and make informed decisions."

Negative Phrase: "Money is always tight."
Positive Reframe: "I am finding ways to increase my financial flexibility and create more abundance."

Negative Phrase: "I'll never be wealthy."
Positive Reframe: "I am committed to creating wealth and taking actions that lead me toward financial success."

Negative Phrase: "I'm stuck in debt."
Positive Reframe: "I am actively working on reducing my debt and building a secure financial future."

5. Use Action-Oriented Language:
Focus on language that emphasises action and progress. Use phrases like "I am taking steps," "I am learning," and "I am making improvements."

6. Visualisation and Affirmations:
Combine positive language with visualisation and affirmations. Visualise your financial success and use affirmations to reinforce your positive beliefs.

7. Practice Self-Awareness:
Be mindful of your language patterns in conversations, both with yourself and others. Catch and correct negative language when you notice it.

8. Surround Yourself with Positivity:
Surround yourself with people who use positive language when discussing money and wealth. Their mindset can influence your own.

9. Journaling:
Keep a journal where you document your positive language patterns, affirmations, and the changes you're making in your financial mindset.

10. Consistency and Patience:
Transforming your language patterns takes time and effort. Be patient and consistent in using positive language.

Using positive language helps shift your focus from limitations to possibilities. By reframing negative phrases into empowering statements, you empower yourself to take proactive steps toward financial success and cultivate a more optimistic and motivated mindset.

Chapter 12 Creating Wealth Rituals

Creating wealth rituals involves establishing daily practices that foster a positive and focused mindset toward wealth creation. These rituals help you stay motivated, maintain consistency, and align your actions with your financial goals. Here's a detailed guide on how to develop wealth rituals that contribute to your financial success:

1. Morning Routine:
Begin your day with positive intentions. Dedicate the first moments of your morning to wealth-related rituals.

2. Affirmations:
Start your day with wealth affirmations that reinforce your positive beliefs about money and abundance.
For example: "I am open to receiving wealth from multiple sources. Today, I take inspired actions toward my financial goals."

3. Visualization:
Set aside time for visualization. Imagine your financial success, visualize achieving your goals, and experience the emotions associated with it.

4. Gratitude Practice:
Express gratitude for the financial resources and opportunities you have. Cultivating a sense of gratitude enhances your overall outlook on wealth.

5. Reading and Learning:
Spend time each day reading wealth-related materials. This could include books, articles, or blogs on personal finance, investing, entrepreneurship, etc.
6. Goal Review:

Review your financial goals daily. Remind yourself of what you're working towards and why it's important to you.

7. Inspired Actions:

Identify small, actionable steps you can take each day to move closer to your financial goals. These actions can be anything from budgeting, saving, investing, to networking.

8. Avoid Negativity:
Eliminate or minimize exposure to negative financial news or discussions that could undermine your positive mindset.

9. Mid-Day Check-In:
Take a few moments during the day to reflect on your financial goals and reaffirm your commitment to your wealth rituals.

10. Evening Reflection:
Review your progress for the day. Acknowledge the steps you took toward your financial goals and celebrate even small wins.

11. Gratitude Before Bed:
End your day by expressing gratitude for the progress you've made and the opportunities you've encountered.

12. Consistency is Key:
The effectiveness of wealth rituals lies in their consistency. Make these practices a non-negotiable part of your daily routine.

13. Flexibility and Adaptability:
Adjust your rituals as needed based on your changing goals and circumstances. What matters is that your rituals remain meaningful to you.

14. Accountability and Support:
Share your wealth rituals with a friend, family member, or accountability partner who can encourage and support you.

15. Track Your Progress:
Keep a journal or digital note of your wealth rituals, experiences, and any shifts in your financial mindset over time.

Developing wealth rituals creates a strong foundation for success by consistently aligning your thoughts, actions, and mindset with your financial goals. These rituals not only keep you focused on wealth creation but also reinforce a positive and empowered relationship with money.

Chapter 13 Neurological Repatterining

Neurological Repatterining using NLP techniques like submodalities involves reshaping the way your brain processes and represents information related to wealth. By modifying the sensory components that accompany your thoughts about money, you can influence your emotional responses and attitudes toward wealth. Here's a detailed guide on how to use submodalities for neurological repatterning:

1. Understanding Submodalities:
Submodalities are the finer distinctions within each of our senses. For example, within the visual sense, submodalities include brightness, size, color, distance, etc.

2. Identify Current Representation:
Identify how you currently represent wealth-related thoughts internally. For example, when you think about money, what images, sounds, and feelings come to mind?

3. Determine the Components:
Break down the representation of wealth-related thoughts into its sensory components—visual, auditory, and kinesthetic (feeling) elements.

4. Modify Submodalities:
Once you've identified the submodalities, you can modify them to change the way you experience these thoughts. Here's how you can do it for each sensory component

Visual Submodalities:
Change the brightness, size, color, or location of the mental image associated with wealth.
For example, if the mental image is dim and distant, make it brighter, larger, and bring it closer.

Auditory Submodalities:
Adjust the volume, tone, or location of any associated sounds related to wealth.

If you hear negative self-talk about money, change the tone to be more encouraging and confident.

Kinesthetic Submodalities:
Modify the intensity, location, or movement of the feelings associated with wealth-related thoughts.
If you feel anxiety or stress when thinking about money, reduce the intensity of those feelings and place them in a more comfortable location in your body.

5. Test and Anchor:
Test the modified submodalities to ensure they feel more positive and empowering.
To anchor the new representation, combine it with a physical touch (e.g., touching two fingers together) or a specific word or gesture that you can use to trigger this positive response.

6. Reinforce with Visualization:
Regularly visualize the modified representation of wealth-related thoughts using the adjusted submodalities.
Engage all your senses in the visualization and experience the positive emotions associated with it.

7. Consistency is Key:
Repetition is crucial for the brain to adopt the new representation. Consistently apply the modified submodalities in your thoughts about money.

8. Monitor Progress:
Keep track of any changes in your feelings, attitudes, and behaviors toward wealth. Notice how your responses evolve over time.
Neurological repatterning through submodalities can help transform your relationship with money by altering how your brain processes and responds to wealth-related thoughts. By consciously modifying the sensory components of these thoughts, you can influence your emotional reactions and foster a more positive and empowered mindset toward wealth and financial success.

Chapter 14 Submodalities

Submodalities are the specific qualities and attributes that make up our sensory experiences. They are the finer distinctions within each of our senses—visual, auditory, kinesthetic, olfactory (smell), and gustatory (taste). Submodalities allow us to process and differentiate various aspects of our sensory perceptions, which in turn influence our thoughts, feelings, and responses. Let's delve into each sensory modality and its corresponding submodalities:

1. Visual Submodalities:
Visual submodalities pertain to how we mentally represent images and scenes in our minds. They include attributes such as:

Brightness: Is the mental image bright or dim?
Size: Is the image large or small?
Color: What colors are present in the image?
Distance: Is the image close or far away?
Location: Where is the image located in your mental space?

2. Auditory Submodalities:
Auditory submodalities involve how we internally process sounds and voices. They encompass attributes like:

Volume: Is the sound loud or soft?
Pitch: Is the sound high-pitched or low-pitched?
Tone: What is the emotional tone of the sound?
Location: Where is the sound coming from?

3. Kinesthetic Submodalities:
Kinesthetic submodalities relate to our sensations and feelings, both physical and emotional. They include attributes such as:

Intensity: How strong or weak is the feeling?
Location: Where do you feel the sensation in your body?
Movement: Is the feeling static or moving?
Temperature: What temperature do you associate with the feeling?

4. Olfactory Submodalities:
Olfactory submodalities concern our internal representations of smells. Attributes here might involve:

Intensity: How strong or faint is the smell?

Quality: What specific scent is associated with the representation?

5. Gustatory Submodalities:
Gustatory submodalities pertain to how we represent tastes in our minds. Attributes might include:

Intensity: How strong or mild is the taste?

Quality: What specific taste is represented?

Using Submodalities in NLP:

In NLP, submodalities are used to explore and modify the sensory components of our thoughts, memories, and experiences. By changing submodalities, individuals can alter their emotional responses, thought patterns, and behaviors. For example, if someone has a negative emotional response to a certain memory, they can modify the submodalities associated with that memory to create a more positive emotional state.

Understanding submodalities provides a powerful tool for changing our internal representations and consequently influencing our thoughts, feelings, and behaviors. By modifying these finer distinctions within our senses, we can shape our perceptions and responses to various stimuli, including those related to money, wealth, and success.

Chapter 15

NLP Exercises to Strengthen New Neural Pathway

Some NLP exercises to help you solidify and strengthen a new neural pathway, making positive changes stick:

1. NLP Exercise: Mirroring and Rapport:

Choose a partner and sit facing each other.

Subtly mirror their body language, gestures, and expressions.

Pay attention to their breathing pace and tone of speech.

Notice how this mirroring helps establish a deeper connection and rapport between you two.

Mirroring and rapport are simple yet powerful techniques that help you connect with others on a deeper level. It's like creating a friendly bond without even saying much!

Here's how it works:

Sit Face to Face: Find a comfortable spot to sit across from someone you want to connect with. It could be a friend, family member, or even a colleague.

Observe and Copy: Pay attention to their body language, gestures, and facial expressions. If they cross their arms, you can subtly cross your arms too. If they take a sip of their drink, you can take a sip too.

Match Their Pace: Try to match their talking speed and tone. If they speak slowly, you can speak a bit slower too. If they sound excited, you can add a little excitement to your voice.

Don't Overdo It: Mirroring isn't about mimicking every move. It's about building a natural connection. So, keep it subtle and genuine.

Pay Attention to Breathing: Notice their breathing rhythm. You don't need to copy it exactly, but being aware of it can help you sync up a bit more.

Why does it work?

When we unconsciously mimic someone's body language and way of speaking, it signals to their brain that you're on the same wavelength. It's like a social cue that says, "Hey, we're similar!" Creating this similarity helps to build trust and rapport. People feel more comfortable around those who seem to understand them. Remember, mirroring is about showing empathy and creating a comfortable atmosphere, not about tricking anyone.
So, the next time you want to connect with someone, give mirroring and rapport a try. It's a simple way to make conversations smoother and friendlier!

2. NLP Exercise: The Swish Pattern

The Swish Pattern is like a superhero move for changing habits or behaviors you want to shake off. It's all about replacing the old habit with a better one, just like swapping your boring sneakers for cool new ones!
Here's how you can do it:

Pick a Habit: Choose a habit you want to change. It could be something like procrastination, nail-biting, or snacking too much.

Picture the Habit: Close your eyes and imagine a picture of yourself doing the old habit. Make it big and clear in your mind.

Create a Better Picture: Now, imagine a smaller, brighter picture of yourself doing a new, positive behavior that you want to adopt. Make this new image really compelling.

SWISH!: In your mind, imagine the small, bright picture growing suddenly and exploding like a firework. As it does, see it replacing the old, big picture.

Repeat the Swish: Do the swish process several times, each time making the new, bright picture more powerful and the old one dimmer.

Practice Often: Practice this exercise every day or whenever you catch yourself falling into the old habit.

Why does it work?

Our brains love excitement and change. The Swish Pattern tricks your brain into getting excited about the new habit, and it makes the old habit seem less appealing. It's like turning the spotlight from the old, boring movie to a new, exciting blockbuster. Remember, changing habits takes time and practice. But with the Swish Pattern, you're giving your brain a cool way to switch gears and choose the better option. So go ahead, give your habits a swish for a positive change!

3. NLP Exercise: Sensory Acuity

Sensory acuity might sound fancy, but it's actually about being a super observer! It's like becoming a detective of body language and expressions.

Here's how you can practice it:

People Watching: Find a comfy spot in a public place, like a park or a café. Sit back and watch people around you.

Pay Attention: Look at how they move, their facial expressions, and how they talk. Notice if they seem happy, tired, excited, or worried.

Body Language: Observe if they cross their arms, tap their feet, or smile a lot. These are like secret messages about how they feel.

Listen Closely: Pay attention to their voices. Are they talking loudly, softly, quickly, or slowly? Do they sound confident or unsure?

Imagine Stories: Use your imagination to guess what might be happening in their lives. Are they meeting a friend, having a bad day, or celebrating something?

Why does it matter?

Sensory acuity helps you understand people better. When you pay attention to their nonverbal cues (like how they move or sound), you can guess their feelings and thoughts. It's like a hidden language that helps you connect with others on a deeper level.

The more you practice, the better you'll become at reading people. And guess what? This skill is super handy in all sorts of situations – like making new friends, talking to teachers, or even working in a team. So, put on your detective hat and start observing the world around you!

4. NLP Exercise: Future Pacing Visualization

Future Pacing Visualization is like creating a movie in your mind about your awesome future. It's a bit like time travel without leaving your chair!
Here's how you can do it:

Find a Quiet Spot: Sit or lie down in a quiet place where you won't be disturbed.

Close Your Eyes: Close your eyes and take a few deep breaths to relax.

Imagine Your Success: Think about a specific goal you want to achieve – like acing a test or landing your dream job.

Create a Movie: Imagine yourself in the future, after you've achieved that goal. Picture it like a movie scene in your mind.

Use All Your Senses: Imagine every detail – what you see, hear, feel, and even smell! Make it as real as possible.

Feel the Emotions: Experience the happiness, pride, and excitement you'll feel when you've accomplished your goal.

Add Action: See yourself taking steps towards your goal. Imagine the actions you'll take and the obstacles you'll overcome.

Stay There for a Moment: Spend a few minutes really living in this successful moment in your mind.

Open Your Eyes: When you're ready, open your eyes and feel the positive energy from your visualization.

Why does it work?

When you vividly imagine your success, it's like telling your brain, "This is where we're headed!" Your brain gets super motivated to make that imagination a reality. It's like giving your future a sneak peek and telling it to get ready for some awesome things.

So, whether it's winning a competition, acing an interview, or nailing a presentation, Future Pacing Visualization helps you get ready for success by painting a clear picture of it in your mind.

5. NLP Exercise: Language reframing

Language reframing is like giving your thoughts a positive makeover. It's about changing the words you use to make things feel better and more hopeful.
Here's how you can do it:

Spot Negative Words: Notice when you say things like "I can't," "I have to," or "It's impossible." These are like rain clouds over your thoughts.

Flip the Script: Change those negative words into positive ones. Instead of "I can't," say "I can learn how to." Instead of "I have to," say "I choose to."

Focus on Solutions: When faced with a problem, instead of saying "I'm stuck," say "I'm finding a way out." It's all about shifting your focus to solutions.

Be Your Cheerleader: Use words that encourage you, like "I'm capable," "I'm determined," and "I've got this!"

Stay Real: While you're changing the words, stay truthful. It's not about pretending everything's perfect, but about focusing on what you can do.
Why does it work?
Our words shape how we see the world and ourselves. When you use positive words, you start to feel more positive too. It's like changing your glasses to see things in a brighter light.
So, the next time you catch yourself using negative words, give them a makeover. Language reframing helps you build a more optimistic and confident mindset, making challenges feel less daunting and more like exciting opportunities!

6. NLP Exercise: Positive Self-Talk

Positive self-talk is like having a supportive friend inside your mind. It's about using kind and encouraging words to boost your confidence and motivation. Here's how you can make positive self-talk a part of your daily life:

Notice Negative Thoughts: Pay attention to the negative thoughts that pop up in your mind. These could be self-doubts, worries, or criticisms.

Challenge Negative Thoughts: Whenever a negative thought arises, question its truthfulness. Is there evidence to support it? Often, negative thoughts are based on assumptions or fears.

Replace with Positive Statements: Once you've challenged the negative thought, replace it with a positive statement. For example, change "I'm not good enough" to "I am capable and improving every day."

Use Encouraging Words: Speak to yourself as you would to a close friend. Use words of kindness, motivation, and support. Imagine what you would say to a friend in a similar situation.

Be Specific: Instead of general positive statements, be specific. For instance, replace "I'll do my best" with "I have the skills and determination to handle this challenge."

Visualize Success: Accompany positive statements with mental images of success. Imagine yourself overcoming obstacles and achieving your goals.

Repeat Regularly: Make positive self-talk a habit. Repeat these affirmations whenever negative thoughts arise or before challenging situations.

Use Present Tense: Phrase your positive statements in the present tense. This helps your mind perceive them as current realities rather than distant goals.

Write Them Down: Write down your positive affirmations in a journal. Reading them regularly reinforces the positive messages.

Practice Patience: Changing thought patterns takes time. Be patient with yourself and understand that it's a gradual process.

Why does it work?
Our thoughts influence our feelings and actions. When you replace negative self-talk with positive affirmations, you're rewiring your brain to focus on solutions, build confidence, and reduce stress. Over time, this positive self-talk becomes a natural way of thinking, boosting your overall mindset and well-being.

7. NLP Exercise: Celebrating Small Wins

Celebrating small wins is like giving yourself a high-five for making progress, no matter how small. It's a way to boost your motivation, build confidence, and stay positive on your journey towards bigger goals. Here's how you can make celebrating small wins a part of your life:

Acknowledge Progress: Notice even the tiniest steps you take towards your goal. It could be completing a task, learning something new, or facing a challenge.

Set Milestones: Break your larger goal into smaller milestones. Each time you reach a milestone, it's a reason to celebrate.

Define Rewards: Associate a reward with each small win. It could be treating yourself to your favorite snack, taking a walk in the park, or watching a movie.

Personalize Rewards: Make sure the rewards resonate with you. They should be something you genuinely enjoy and look forward to.

Pause and Reflect: When you achieve a small win, take a moment to reflect on the effort you put in and the progress you've made.

Share with Others: Let friends, family, or colleagues know about your small wins. Their positive reactions can amplify your sense of accomplishment.

Keep a Wins Journal: Maintain a journal where you document your small wins. Reading through it can remind you of how far you've come.

Celebrate Mindfully: When you celebrate, be present in the moment. Fully enjoy the reward and the sense of achievement.

Use Positive Self-Talk: Tell yourself, "I did it!" or "I'm making progress!" Positive self-talk reinforces the feeling of accomplishment.

Stay Consistent: Make celebrating small wins a habit. Regularly acknowledging progress keeps you motivated and engaged.

Why does it work?

Celebrating small wins reinforces positive behavior. When you acknowledge your efforts and achievements, your brain releases chemicals like dopamine that create a sense of happiness and satisfaction. This positive reinforcement strengthens your motivation and encourages you to keep moving forward. Over time, these small celebrations build up and contribute to your overall sense of achievement and success.

8. NLP Exercise: Creating a Visualization Board

Creating a visualization board is like making a visual roadmap of your dreams and goals. It's a fun and creative way to keep your aspirations in front of you, reminding you of what you're working towards. Here's how you can create your own visualization board:

Gather Your Supplies:

Get a poster board, corkboard, or even a digital platform where you can assemble your visual elements.

Collect magazines, newspapers, images, quotes, and any other materials that resonate with your goals.

Clarify Your Goals:

Before you start, be clear about your goals. What do you want to achieve? It could be related to career, health, relationships, or personal growth.

Choose Your Focus:

Decide if you want a board that covers all your goals or one that focuses on a specific area of your life.

Select Visuals:

Flip through magazines and find images, words, and quotes that represent your goals and dreams.

Choose visuals that resonate with you emotionally and make you feel excited.

Arrange and Assemble:

Arrange your visuals on the board in a way that makes sense to you. You can organize them by theme or let your creativity flow freely.

Add Personal Touches:

Include personal photos, handwritten notes, or drawings that hold special meaning for you.

Visualize and Feel:

Spend time looking at your board regularly.
As you do, close your eyes and imagine yourself living the life depicted on the board. Feel the emotions associated with achieving your goals.

Place It Prominently:

Put your visualization board in a place where you'll see it daily – on your bedroom wall, near your workspace, or as the wallpaper on your digital device.

Update and Evolve:

Your goals and aspirations might change over time. Feel free to update your board whenever you have new dreams to pursue.

Stay Inspired:

Let your visualization board serve as a source of inspiration and motivation on your journey towards your goals.

Why does it work?
Visualization boards make your goals tangible. By surrounding yourself with images and words that represent your desires, you're constantly reminding yourself of what you're working towards. Visualization activates your imagination and emotions, aligning your subconscious mind with your conscious goals. It helps you stay focused, motivated, and excited about your journey to success.

9. NLP Exercise: Mindful Integration

Mindful integration is like weaving a sense of presence into your daily activities. It's about being fully engaged in the moment, which can lead to better focus, reduced stress, and a deeper connection with what you're doing. Here's how you can practice mindful integration:

Choose an Activity: Select a routine activity you often do, like washing dishes, taking a shower, or eating a meal.

Set Your Intention: Before you start, remind yourself that you're going to fully engage in this activity with mindfulness.

Focus on Your Senses: As you engage in the activity, pay attention to your senses. Notice the sensations, textures, smells, and sounds involved.

Stay Present: If your mind starts to wander, gently bring your focus back to the activity. It's okay if your mind drifts – the practice is in redirecting your attention.

Avoid Multitasking: Dedicate your full attention to the chosen activity. Don't try to do other tasks or check your phone simultaneously.

Breathe Mindfully: Use your breath as an anchor. Whenever your mind wanders, take a deep breath and return to the present moment.

Engage Your Senses: Engage with the activity using all your senses. Feel the water on your hands, savor the flavors of your meal, or appreciate the warmth of the shower.

Let Go of Judgment: Practice non-judgmental awareness. Don't label things as good or bad – simply observe them as they are.

Extend to Other Activities: As you become comfortable with one activity, start integrating mindfulness into other parts of your day.

Be Patient: Mindful integration takes practice. It's normal for your mind to wander, but the more you practice, the better you'll become at staying present.

Why does it work?

Mindful integration helps you break free from autopilot mode and experience each moment with intention. By focusing on the present, you reduce stress, anxiety, and negative rumination. It also cultivates a greater appreciation for the simple joys in life. With practice, you'll find that you can carry the mindful awareness cultivated during integration into other areas of your life, leading to a more mindful and fulfilling existence.

Some Daily Simple Exercises

There are a few more exercises to help you change neural pathways and promote positive changes in your mindset and behavior:

Gratitude Journaling:

Each day, write down three things you're grateful for.
This exercise shifts your focus to the positive aspects of your life, rewiring your brain to notice and appreciate the good.

Visualization with Emotion:

Close your eyes and vividly imagine achieving a goal.
As you do this, engage your emotions. Feel the excitement, joy, and satisfaction as if you've already succeeded.

Three Good Things:

Before bed, recall three good things that happened during the day.
This exercise trains your brain to focus on positive experiences and cultivates a more optimistic outlook.

Mindful Breathing:

Take a few minutes to focus solely on your breath.
This simple practice reduces stress and rewires your brain for better focus and emotional regulation.

Random Acts of Kindness:

Do something kind for someone without expecting anything in return.
Acts of kindness release feel-good chemicals in your brain, reinforcing positive behaviors.

Daily Affirmations:

Repeat positive affirmations every morning.

This exercise rewires your brain to embrace self-belief and confidence.

Challenge Negative Thoughts:

When negative thoughts arise, question their validity.

This exercise helps break the cycle of automatic negative thinking.

Learn a New Skill:

Pick up a hobby or skill you've never tried before.

Learning something new creates new neural connections and enhances cognitive flexibility.

Physical Exercise:

Engage in regular physical activity.

Exercise increases blood flow to the brain, boosting cognitive function and mood.

Meditation:

Practice mindfulness meditation to calm your mind and improve focus.

Meditation rewires your brain for emotional regulation and reduces stress.

Limit Multitasking:

Focus on one task at a time.

This practice strengthens your ability to concentrate and boosts productivity.

Remember, changing neural pathways takes time and consistent effort. Incorporate these exercises into your daily routine and be patient with yourself. Over time, these positive practices can lead to lasting changes in your thoughts, emotions, and behaviors.

Part II

ADVANCED NLP FOR WEALTH

Advanced NLP Practices

Moving beyond the basics of Neuro-Linguistic Programming (NLP), advanced NLP practices represent a deeper dive into the intricacies of the human mind and communication. These techniques are specifically crafted to facilitate profound personal transformation, enhance communication skills, and enable individuals to achieve specific life goals with greater finesse and precision. In this advanced realm of NLP, practitioners explore the multifaceted layers of consciousness and the subtle nuances of language to effect profound shifts in their thinking, behavior, and interactions with others. These practices are not only tools for personal growth but also keys to unlocking the vast potential of the human mind.

Some advanced NLP practices that go beyond the basics:

Submodality Swish Pattern:

> Modify the submodalities (sensory components) of an undesirable behavior or emotion in your mind.
>
> Then use the "swish" technique to replace it with a desired behavior or emotion that has enhanced submodalities.

Parts Integration:

> Identify conflicting parts of yourself that have different goals or desires.
>
> Use NLP techniques to facilitate a dialogue and find common ground between these parts.

Six-Step Reframing:

> Explore the positive intention behind a behavior or habit you want to change.
>
> Work through a six-step process that involves reframing the behavior and finding alternative ways to fulfill the positive intention.

Belief Change Patterns:

Explore and transform limiting beliefs that hold you back. Techniques like "New Behavior Generator" or "Changing Personal History" help reframe your belief system.

TimeLine Therapy:

Work with your internal timeline to release negative emotions and limiting decisions from the past.
Create a compelling future by installing positive emotions and beliefs.

Nested Loops:

Use storytelling and layered metaphors to lead someone's mind through a series of intertwined stories.
This technique can create a deep impact on the listener's subconscious mind.

Reimprinting:

Revisit past memories and reimprint them with positive emotions and perspectives.
This can be particularly useful for resolving past traumas or negative experiences.

Advanced Anchoring:

Combine anchors to create complex emotional states.
For instance, you can anchor confidence, motivation, and excitement together for a specific context.

Metaprograms:

Understand and influence the filters through which people perceive the world.
Adapt your communication style to resonate with different metaprogram preferences.

Advanced Language Patterns:

Utilize Milton Model language patterns for indirect communication and persuasion.

Employ complex language structures to influence and build rapport.

These advanced NLP practices require a deeper understanding of NLP principles and more experience. If you're interested in exploring these techniques, consider working with an experienced NLP practitioner or undergoing advanced NLP training.

1. The Submodality Swish Pattern

The Submodality Swish Pattern is an advanced NLP technique used to shift your perceptions and associations with certain experiences, thoughts, or feelings. By modifying the submodalities (finer distinctions within our senses) of your mental representations, you can change the way you respond to specific stimuli. When applied to enhancing your wealth mindset, the Submodality Swish Pattern can help you transform negative associations with wealth-related thoughts into positive and empowering ones. Here's how to use the Submodality Swish Pattern for enhancing your relationship with wealth:

1. Identify the Target State and Desired State:
Determine the negative thought or association related to wealth that you want to transform (target state). Also, identify the positive and empowering thought or belief about wealth that you want to replace it with (desired state).

2. Access the Target State:
Recall the negative thought or association related to wealth. As you do this, notice the submodalities associated with this thought, such as the images, sounds, feelings, and sensations that accompany it.

3. Create a Swish Image:
Create a clear mental image of the positive and empowering thought about wealth (desired state). Make sure this image is bright, vivid, and compelling.

4. Make the Swish:
In your mind, imagine the Swish Image as a small thumbnail-sized picture in the bottom left corner of your mental space. At the same time, see the negative image (target state) as a larger, faded image in the center of your mental space.

5. Amplify the Swish Image:
Quickly and suddenly expand the Swish Image from the bottom left corner to cover and replace the negative image (target state). Imagine it growing bigger, brighter, and more vibrant until it completely overlays the negative image.

6. Use Submodalities:
During the swish, adjust the submodalities of the images to intensify the change. For example, make the Swish Image brighter, closer, larger, and more colorful, while making the negative image dimmer, smaller, and less distinct.

7. Repeat and Automate:
Repeat the swish several times, ensuring that the Swish Image replaces the negative image each time. Speed up the process until it feels automatic and effortless.

8. Break State:
Take a moment to clear your mind and break the pattern. This helps to separate yourself from the old negative association.

9. Test and Reinforce:
Test the swish by intentionally bringing up the old negative thought about wealth. Notice if the Swish Image automatically replaces it with the positive desired state. If needed, repeat the process to reinforce the change.
10. Anchor the Positive State:
Create an anchor (a physical touch or gesture) that you can use to trigger the positive desired state whenever you think about wealth. This reinforces the new association over time.
Using the Submodality Swish Pattern allows you to rewire your subconscious associations with wealth-related thoughts, replacing negative patterns with positive and empowering ones. Consistency and practice are key to making this technique effective in shifting your wealth mindset.

2. Parts Integration

Parts Integration is an advanced NLP technique used to resolve internal conflicts between different parts of yourself that have conflicting goals or desires. In the context of wealth, you can use this technique to harmonize conflicting beliefs, attitudes, or emotions related to money and financial success. Here's a detailed guide on how to apply Parts Integration for enhancing your relationship with wealth:

Step 1: Identify the Conflicting Parts:
Identify the conflicting parts of yourself related to wealth. These could be opposing beliefs, emotions, or attitudes.
For example, one part might desire financial abundance, while another part fears the responsibilities that come with wealth.

Step 2: Establish Communication:
Imagine that these conflicting parts are characters in a play. Give each part a voice and personality.
Mentally step into each part and have a dialogue between them.
Let each part express its concerns and intentions.

Step 3: Identify Positive Intentions:
Understand that each conflicting part has a positive intention. Even if their approaches differ, they both want something good for you.
Identify the positive intentions behind each part's desires related to wealth.

Step 4: Find Common Ground:
Facilitate a conversation between the conflicting parts to find common ground or shared goals.
Encourage them to collaborate and find a way to achieve their positive intentions together.

Step 5: Integrate the Parts:
Imagine bringing the two conflicting parts together. You might visualize them merging or shaking hands.
Feel a sense of unity and harmony between these parts.

Step 6: Test Integration:
After the integration, observe how you feel about wealth-related thoughts and situations.
Ideally, you should feel a greater sense of alignment and coherence in your attitudes toward wealth.

Step 7: Reinforce and Practice:
Regularly remind yourself of the integration and the common goals of the previously conflicting parts.
If any conflicts arise, use this technique to address them promptly.

Remember that Parts Integration can be a profound process, but it may require deep introspection and self-awareness. This technique is most effective when facilitated by an experienced NLP practitioner, especially if you're new to advanced NLP practices.
By harmonizing conflicting internal voices, you can create a more unified and positive mindset toward wealth and financial success.

3. The Six-Step Reframing

The Six-Step Reframing is an advanced NLP technique used to uncover the positive intention behind a behavior or habit you want to change and find alternative ways to fulfill that intention. In the context of wealth, you can use this technique to explore and transform any negative behaviors or attitudes related to money. Here's a detailed guide on how to apply the Six-Step Reframing process for enhancing your relationship with wealth:

Step 1: Identify the Behavior:
Identify the negative behavior or attitude related to wealth that you want to change. It could be overspending, avoiding financial planning, or feeling guilty about money.

Step 2: Separate the Intention:
Recognize that every behavior, even negative ones, have a positive intention behind them.
Separate the intention from the behavior. For example, overspending might be an attempt to seek enjoyment or fulfillment.

Step 3: Find Alternative Behaviors:
Brainstorm alternative behaviors that can fulfill the same positive intention in healthier ways.
For example, if overspending seeks enjoyment, alternative behaviors could include finding affordable ways to have fun or engaging in hobbies.

Step 4: Ecological Check:
Consider the potential consequences of the alternative behaviors. Ensure they align with your overall well-being and values.
Make sure the alternatives are sustainable and don't lead to other negative outcomes.

Step 5: Future Pacing:
Mentally project yourself into the future and imagine implementing the alternative behaviors.
Observe how these new behaviors positively impact your relationship with wealth and financial well-being.

Step 6: Reintegration and Test:
Reconnect with the initial negative behavior and acknowledge its positive intention.
Mentally integrate the awareness of alternative behaviors and their positive outcomes.
Notice how your perspective toward the negative behavior has shifted.

Step 7: Reinforce and Practice:
Regularly remind yourself of the alternative behaviors and their positive intentions.
Whenever the negative behavior arises, consciously choose to implement the alternatives.

Remember that the Six-Step Reframing process can lead to profound shifts in your mindset and behavior related to wealth. It's recommended to work with an experienced NLP practitioner when applying advanced techniques like this, especially if you're new to NLP practices. By understanding and addressing the positive intentions behind your behaviors, you can transform your relationship with wealth and cultivate healthier financial habits.

4. Belief Change Patterns

Advanced Belief Change Patterns in NLP specifically for enhancing your relationship with wealth:

Step 1: Belief Elicitation:
Start by identifying the specific limiting beliefs you hold about wealth. These could be ingrained thoughts like "I'll never be rich" or "Money is the root of all problems."

Step 2: Meta-Modeling:
Apply the Meta-Model questioning technique to challenge and unpack these beliefs. For instance, ask, "How do you know you'll never be rich?" or "What specifically makes money the root of all problems?"

Step 3: Reframe and Challenge:
Reframe the limiting beliefs into open-ended questions that challenge their assumptions. For example, change "I can't make a lot of money" to "How can I increase my financial abundance?"

Step 4: Counterexamples:
Explore counterexamples to your limiting beliefs. Look for instances where your belief doesn't hold true.
For instance, if you believe "Money is hard to come by," find examples of people who have achieved financial success relatively easily.

Step 5: Submodalities Exploration:
Dive deeper into the submodalities (sensory qualities) of your limiting beliefs. Identify the sensory components of the belief, such as its location, size, brightness, and associated emotions.
Step 6: Submodalities Change:

Modify the submodalities of your limiting beliefs to reduce their impact. For instance, make the image of the belief smaller, dimmer, and move it further away in your mind.

Simultaneously, enhance the submodalities of an empowering belief related to wealth. Make this image brighter, larger, and closer.

Step 7: Anchoring Empowering States:
Anchor the positive emotions associated with your empowering belief to a physical anchor, such as pressing your thumb and forefinger together.
Use this anchor to access the empowering emotional state whenever you want to shift your mindset.

Step 8: Future Pacing:
Mentally project yourself into the future where you've already integrated the empowering belief about wealth.
Imagine the positive impact it has on your financial decisions, actions, and outcomes.

Step 9: Test and Integration:
Test your new empowering belief by deliberately thinking about wealth-related scenarios.
Observe how your emotions and attitudes have shifted toward a more positive and empowering perspective.

Step 10: Reinforce and Practice:
Continuously practice this belief change pattern by integrating it into your daily routine.
Regularly visualize, anchor, and reinforce your empowering belief.

Remember that belief change takes time and repetition. These advanced Belief Change Patterns are potent tools for transforming your mindset around wealth, but they require commitment and practice. If you're new to advanced NLP techniques, seeking guidance from an experienced practitioner can provide valuable support on your journey to changing your relationship with wealth.

5. TimeLine Therapy

TimeLine Therapy is an advanced NLP technique used to release negative emotions, limiting decisions, and unresolved issues from the past, allowing you to create a compelling and empowered future. In the context of wealth, this technique can help you remove emotional barriers related to money and open yourself to greater abundance. Here's a detailed guide on how to apply TimeLine Therapy for enhancing your relationship with wealth:

Step 1: Set Clear Intentions:
Clearly define the specific emotional barriers or limiting beliefs related to wealth that you want to address.
Set a positive intention for releasing these barriers and creating a prosperous mindset.

Step 2: Prepare for the Process:
Find a quiet and comfortable space where you won't be disturbed.
Mentally prepare yourself for a deep exploration of your emotions and past experiences.

Step 3: Access Your TimeLine:
Close your eyes and imagine a line representing your TimeLine, extending from your past to your future.
Locate the point on the TimeLine where your negative emotions or limiting beliefs related to wealth might have originated.

Step 4: Step into the Memory:
Mentally step into the memory associated with the negative emotion or limiting belief.
Re-experience the emotions and feelings associated with that memory.

Step 5: Release and Heal:
As you re-experience the memory, use your imagination to release the negative emotions and beliefs from that experience.
Imagine them leaving your body and dissipating into the air.

Step 6: Replace with Empowering Beliefs:
Once the negative emotions are released, fill the space with empowering beliefs related to wealth.
Visualize yourself integrating these positive beliefs at the same memory point.

Step 7: Create a Compelling Future:
Mentally move along your TimeLine to the present day and then into the future.
Imagine your life with these new empowering beliefs around wealth. Visualize your financial success and abundance.

Step 8: Reinforce and Integrate:
Regularly practice TimeLine Therapy to ensure the integration of your new beliefs.
Visualize your compelling future and reinforce your empowered mindset daily.
Step 9: Seek Professional Guidance:
TimeLine Therapy can be deeply emotional and impactful. If you're dealing with significant emotional traumas or complex issues, consider working with a certified TimeLine Therapy practitioner.

Remember that TimeLine Therapy can bring about profound shifts in your emotional state and beliefs. It's a technique that requires sincere introspection and self-awareness. Practicing this technique consistently can help you release emotional blocks related to wealth and create a more abundant and prosperous mindset.

6. Nested Loops

Nested Loops is an advanced NLP technique used for storytelling and communication that involves embedding multiple layers of stories or metaphors within each other. In the context of wealth, Nested Loops can be used to communicate and influence positively about wealth-related topics in a way that engages the listener's subconscious mind. Here's a detailed guide on how to apply Nested Loops for enhancing your relationship with wealth:

Step 1: Define the Main Message:
Determine the main message or positive idea you want to convey related to wealth. It could be about abundance, financial freedom, or success.

Step 2: Create a Story Loop:
Craft a compelling story or metaphor that illustrates your main message about wealth.
Ensure that this story has a clear structure with a beginning, middle, and end.

Step 3: Introduce the Nested Loop:
Within your main story, introduce a secondary story or metaphor related to wealth that supports the main message.
This secondary story can be subtly intertwined with the main story.

Step 4: Transition and Suspend:
Transition smoothly from the main story to the nested story.
Suspend the main story without a clear conclusion, keeping the listener engaged and curious.

Step 5: Develop the Nested Story:
Dive into the nested story, exploring its characters, events, and lessons.

Ensure that the nested story aligns with and reinforces the main message.

Step 6: Loop Back to the Main Story:
After developing the nested story, loop back to the main story without completing it.
Refer back to the main message and remind the listener of its relevance.

Step 7: Conclude and Deliver the Message:
Conclude the nested story with a powerful message that echoes the main message about wealth.
Reinforce the positive ideas related to wealth, abundance, or success.

Step 8: Allow the Impact to Settle:
Give the listener some space to reflect on the stories and messages.
This allows the subconscious mind to absorb and process the positive ideas about wealth.

Step 9: Repeat if Necessary:
Depending on the complexity of the message, you can create multiple nested loops to layer the impact.
However, be mindful not to overcomplicate the communication.

Step 10: Practice and Refine:
Practice delivering nested loops with natural flow and timing.
Pay attention to the engagement and reactions of your audience.

Nested Loops can be powerful tools for communicating ideas about wealth in a way that engages both the conscious and subconscious mind. This technique requires storytelling skills and practice to effectively convey your message and create a positive impact related to wealth and prosperity.

An example of a nested loop using an advanced NLP storytelling technique to convey a positive message about wealth:

Main Message: Embracing an Abundant Mindset Leads to Wealth

Main Story:

Imagine a young traveler named John who embarked on a journey to a distant land seeking his fortune. Along the way, he faced challenges, met interesting characters, and learned valuable lessons. As he navigated through twists and turns, he discovered an old sage known for his wisdom.

Nested Loop:
Nested Story:
The sage began to share a story of a hidden garden. In this garden, every tree bore golden fruit. People from all over would visit, and their buckets would overflow with the golden harvest. Yet, there was one condition: they had to enter with an open heart and gratitude.

Back to Main Story:
John was captivated by the sage's words. He realized that the garden symbolized the mind, and the golden fruit represented opportunities for wealth. The sage explained that those who approach life with an open heart and gratitude, like the garden visitors, attract abundant opportunities.

Nested Loop Continues:
Nested Story:
The sage went on to share another tale about a skilled archer who aimed for a distant target. With each shot, he visualized success, believing that the arrow had already hit its mark. Miraculously, his arrows always found their target.

Back to Main Story:
John connected this story with the previous one. He understood that just like the archer, having a clear vision of wealth and success, and believing it's already achieved, can attract wealth and opportunities.

Nested Loop Conclusion:
Nested Story:
The sage's final story was of a sculptor who turned blocks of stone into magnificent statues. Each sculpture began as an idea in his mind. With each chisel strike, he brought his vision to life, revealing the hidden beauty within the stone.

Back to Main Story:
John realized that he, too, could sculpt his wealth through focused actions and a positive mindset. He learned that his mind was like the sculptor's stone, waiting to be shaped into a masterpiece of abundance.

Final Message:
As John bid farewell to the sage, he understood that embracing an abundant mindset, visualizing success, and taking focused actions were the keys to unlocking wealth and prosperity. Just as the hidden garden, the skilled archer, and the sculptor had shown him, wealth wasn't just about money; it was about shaping his thoughts and actions to create a life of abundance.
In this example, the main message about embracing an abundant mindset leading to wealth is conveyed through a series of nested stories. Each story illustrates a different aspect of the message, reinforcing the idea from different angles and engaging the listener's subconscious mind. This technique encourages the listener to reflect on the stories and internalize the message about wealth and abundance.

Another example of a nested loop using an advanced NLP storytelling technique:

Nested Loop: The Journey of Abundance

Once upon a time, in a small village, there lived a young woman named Monica. Monica was known for her wisdom and her deep understanding of the power of the mind. One day, she decided to share her wisdom with the villagers in a special gathering.

As the villagers gathered around, Monica began to tell a tale about a journey. "Imagine," she said, "that you are embarking on a journey through a magical forest. This forest is abundant, filled with lush trees, sparkling streams, and vibrant flowers."

Nested Loop Layer 1: The Power of Perception
"In this forest," Monica continued, "the way you perceive things shapes your experience. Just like in life, how you perceive abundance will influence what you attract. If you see scarcity, you'll find scarcity. But if you see abundance, you'll find opportunities everywhere."

Nested Loop Layer 2: The Mirror of Beliefs
"Now, on this journey, you come across a mystical mirror," Monica went on. "This mirror reflects your beliefs about wealth and success. As you gaze into it, ask yourself: What beliefs are holding me back? Are they truly mine, or have they been passed down?"

Nested Loop Layer 1: Return to the Forest
"As you move deeper into the forest," Monica resumed, "remember the power of perception. See the trees as symbols of growth and potential. See the streams as a reminder of the constant flow of opportunities. And see the flowers as evidence of the beauty that surrounds you."

Nested Loop Layer 2: Planting Seeds of Intention

"Then, you stumble upon a clearing," Monica continued. "In this clearing, you can plant seeds of intention. Each seed represents a goal or desire related to wealth. Just as you nurture these seeds, nurture your intentions with focused actions."

Nested Loop Layer 1: The Abundant Path

"Back on the path," Monica reminded, "embrace the abundant path you've chosen. Your perceptions and beliefs are guiding you. Every step you take, every decision you make, is a step toward a more prosperous life."

Nested Loop Layer 2: Harvest of Mindset

"Finally," Monica concluded, "as you exit the forest, you find yourself in a field of harvest. This harvest represents the rewards of your mindset and actions. It's a reflection of the abundance you've cultivated within."

Nested Loop Layer 1: Return to Reality

As Monica finished her tale, she looked around at the captivated villagers. "Remember," she said, "that the journey through the forest is a journey within. The power to change your perception and beliefs lies within you. Embrace abundance, plant seeds of intention, and harvest the rewards of your empowered mindset."

And so, the villagers left the gathering with a renewed understanding of their power to shape their own realities and create a life filled with abundance.

In this nested loop, the main story about Monica sharing her wisdom is interwoven with the layers of the forest journey and the mirror of beliefs. Each layer reinforces the main message while adding depth and complexity to the storytelling experience, a technique often used in advanced NLP to engage and influence listeners on multiple levels.

7. ReImprinting

ReImprinting is an advanced NLP technique used to transform past negative experiences and replace them with new, empowering perspectives. In the context of wealth, ReImprinting can help you identify and reframe any early negative experiences or beliefs related to money, allowing you to create a more positive and abundant relationship with wealth. Here's a detailed guide on how to apply ReImprinting for enhancing your wealth mindset:

Step 1: Identify Early Negative Experiences:
Reflect on your past and identify any significant negative experiences or memories related to money, abundance, or wealth. These experiences might have influenced your current beliefs and attitudes about money.

Step 2: Access the Memory:
Choose one of the identified memories and recall it vividly. Immerse yourself in the memory, experiencing the emotions, thoughts, and sensations associated with it.

Step 3: Resourceful State:
Before beginning the reimprinting process, access a resourceful state. Recall a time when you felt confident, empowered, and positive.
Anchor this resourceful state by touching your thumb and forefinger together.

Step 4: Enter the Memory:
Step back into the memory as an observer. See yourself in the memory as if you're watching a movie.
Maintain the resourceful state and the anchored touch.

Step 5: Change the Memory:
Begin to change the memory by introducing positive elements. For example, imagine a supportive mentor or a wise version of yourself offering guidance.
Alter the events, dialogue, or outcome of the memory to create a positive, empowering scenario.

Step 6: Absorb the Positive Experience:
Step into the altered memory and fully experience the positive emotions, thoughts, and sensations.
Allow these positive feelings to become an integral part of the memory.

Step 7: Future Pacing:
Imagine how your life would have been different if you had experienced the positive version of the memory.
Visualize how this new perspective would have influenced your beliefs and actions related to wealth.

Step 8: Release and ReImprint:
Gradually step out of the memory, leaving behind the old negative emotions and beliefs.
Bring the positive emotions and beliefs from the ReImprinted memory into your present self.

Step 9: Integrate and Practice:
Regularly reflect on the ReImprinted memory and the positive beliefs associated with it.
Whenever you encounter situations related to wealth, recall the new perspective and apply it.

Step 10: Seek Professional Guidance:
ReImprinting can be emotionally intense, especially when dealing with significant past experiences. If you're working through deep-seated issues, consider working with a certified NLP practitioner.

ReImprinting empowers you to rewrite the narrative of your past and transform it into a positive force for your wealth mindset. By changing your early associations and beliefs about money, you can create a more empowering relationship with wealth and abundance.

8. Advanced Anchoring

Advanced Anchoring is an NLP technique used to associate specific emotions, states, or behaviors with anchors that can be triggered later to recreate those experiences. In the context of wealth, Advanced Anchoring can help you access and maintain a mindset of abundance and prosperity. Here's a detailed guide on how to apply Advanced Anchoring for enhancing your wealth mindset:

Step 1: Choose Resourceful States:
Identify the resourceful states you want to anchor related to wealth, such as confidence, motivation, or a sense of abundance.
Recall times when you felt these states strongly.

Step 2: Set Up Anchors:
Choose a unique physical anchor, such as pressing your thumb and forefinger together, for each resourceful state.
Ensure your anchor is consistent and distinct.

Step 3: Access Resourceful States:
Relax and recall a memory or imagine a situation where you experienced one of the resourceful states.
Fully immerse yourself in the memory, re-experiencing the emotions and sensations.

Step 4: Fire the Anchor:
At the peak of the emotional state, trigger the chosen anchor (press your thumb and forefinger together).
Repeat this process several times to strengthen the association between the anchor and the emotional state.

Step 5: Test and Reinforce:
Test the anchor by triggering it while not in the emotional state. You should feel the emotions associated with the anchor.
If the anchor isn't strong enough, repeat the process, intensifying the emotions each time.

Step 6: Stack Anchors:
You can stack multiple anchors for different resourceful states related to wealth.
For instance, you might have separate anchors for confidence, motivation, and abundance.

Step 7: Apply in Relevant Situations:
Whenever you want to access a specific resourceful state, trigger the corresponding anchor.
Use these anchors before important financial decisions, goal-setting sessions, or times when you need a wealth mindset.

Step 8: Future Pacing:
Imagine yourself in future situations requiring a wealth mindset. Trigger the anchors to mentally and emotionally prepare yourself for success.

Step 9: Maintenance and Refinement:
Regularly reinforce the anchors by triggering them and accessing the associated resourceful states.
If needed, fine-tune the anchors to ensure their effectiveness.

Step 10: Seek Professional Guidance:
Advanced Anchoring can be intricate and may require guidance to achieve optimal results.
Working with an experienced NLP practitioner can help you refine your anchoring techniques.

By using Advanced Anchoring techniques, you can create a toolbox of resourceful states that empower you to navigate wealth-related situations with confidence, motivation, and an abundance mindset. These anchored emotions can contribute to making more aligned and positive financial decisions.

9. Metaprograms

Metaprograms are cognitive patterns or mental filters that shape how individuals perceive, process, and respond to information and experiences. They are the higher-level mental programs that influence our thoughts, behaviors, and decision-making processes. Metaprograms go beyond individual preferences and are more about how people generally organize and make sense of the world around them.

In essence, metaprograms are like mental shortcuts that our brains use to process vast amounts of information efficiently. They help us filter, categorize, and prioritize information based on our internal programming. Metaprograms operate at an unconscious level, influencing our perceptions and actions without us being fully aware of their impact.

Here are a few common examples of metaprograms:

Towards-Away: This metaprogram determines whether a person is motivated by moving towards positive outcomes or by moving away from negative ones. Some people are more focused on pursuing rewards, while others are more motivated to avoid risks or problems.

Internal-External: This metaprogram reflects whether a person's focus and evaluation come from within themselves (internal) or from external sources (external). Internal individuals rely more on their personal values and beliefs, while external individuals pay more attention to external feedback.

Options-Procedures: This metaprogram relates to how a person approaches tasks. Some individuals prefer exploring various options before making decisions (options), while others prefer following established steps and procedures (procedures).

Toward-Away Time Frame: This metaprogram indicates whether a person is more future-oriented (toward) or past-oriented (away). Future-oriented individuals focus on possibilities and goals, while past-oriented individuals may emphasize lessons from the past.

Big Chunk-Small Chunk: This metaprogram determines whether a person tends to focus on the bigger picture (big chunk) or on details (small chunk) when processing information.

Sameness-Difference: This metaprogram reflects how a person perceives similarities and differences between things. Some individuals notice and appreciate distinctions, while others see commonalities.

Understanding metaprograms can provide valuable insights into how people think, make decisions, and communicate. In the context of personal development, including wealth mindset enhancement, recognizing your own metaprogram tendencies and those of others can help you tailor your strategies for effective communication, decision-making, and goal achievement.

Let’s understand it in another way;

Metaprograms in NLP are mental patterns or filters that influence how individuals perceive and respond to the world around them. Understanding and utilizing metaprograms can provide insights into someone's motivations, preferences, and decision-making processes. When it comes to wealth, recognizing and leveraging metaprograms can help you tailor your approach to align with your financial goals. Here's a detailed guide on how to apply Metaprograms for enhancing your wealth mindset:

Step 1: Identify Relevant Metaprograms:

Learn about various metaprograms, such as Towards-Away, Internal-External, Options-Procedures, etc.
Identify the metaprograms that are most relevant to your wealth mindset and financial goals.

Step 2: Self-Assessment:
Reflect on your own tendencies and preferences in terms of the identified metaprograms.
For example, do you tend to focus more on the benefits of wealth (Towards) or on avoiding financial problems (Away)?

Step 3: Understand Others:
Apply your knowledge of metaprograms to understand how other people perceive and approach wealth.
This can help you communicate effectively and tailor your message to their preferences.

Step 4: Adjust Your Communication:
When discussing wealth-related matters, adapt your communication style based on the other person's metaprogram preferences.
Use language and examples that resonate with their tendencies.

Step 5: Align with Your Goals:
Utilize metaprograms to align your actions and decisions with your wealth goals.
For example, if you tend to focus on the positive outcomes (Towards), consistently visualize and work toward those outcomes.

Step 6: Flexibility in Approach:
Be flexible in your approach to wealth-related situations, understanding that different metaprograms may require different strategies.
Adapt your mindset and actions based on the specific circumstances.

Step 7: Recognize Patterns:
Pay attention to patterns of behavior and responses in yourself and others related to wealth.
Identify recurring metaprogram tendencies and adjust your strategies accordingly.

Step 8: Seek Professional Insights:
If you're new to metaprograms, consider working with an experienced NLP practitioner to gain deeper insights and guidance.
They can provide personalized assessments and strategies tailored to your metaprogram tendencies.

Step 9: Continuous Reflection and Improvement:
Continuously reflect on how metaprograms influence your thoughts and behaviors related to wealth.
Regularly refine your strategies based on your evolving understanding.

Understanding and applying metaprograms can enhance your ability to communicate effectively, align your actions with your wealth goals, and develop a more attuned mindset for financial success. By recognizing the unique ways individuals approach wealth, you can build stronger connections, make more informed decisions, and enhance your overall wealth mindset.

Advanced Language Patterns

Advanced Language Patterns

Advanced language patterns in NLP can be powerful tools to influence and shape the way you think and approach wealth. These patterns leverage linguistic structures and techniques to communicate more effectively with your subconscious mind. Here are some advanced language patterns tailored for enhancing your wealth mindset:

1. Hypnotic Language:
Utilize language that engages the subconscious mind, such as:
"As you listen to these words, you'll find your wealth mindset deepening."
"Imagine yourself effortlessly attracting wealth into your life."

2. Embedded Commands:
Hide commands within sentences to influence your mindset:
"You can start taking steps toward wealth now."
"Notice how your thoughts about wealth are becoming more positive."

3. Presuppositions:
Phrase sentences that presuppose certain beliefs or states:
"When you begin to view wealth as a natural outcome of your efforts..."
"As you explore various ways to create abundance..."

4. Time-Related Language:
Incorporate time-related language to evoke a sense of progress:
"Soon, you'll discover new avenues for financial growth."
"With each passing day, your wealth mindset becomes stronger."

5. Cause and Effect:
Link actions and thoughts to desired outcomes:

"When you consistently focus on abundance, your actions align with wealth creation."
"By adopting these beliefs, you set in motion a chain of prosperous events."

6. Analogical Framing:
Use analogies to convey complex concepts:
"Just as a gardener tends to plants, you nurture your financial goals."
"Think of your wealth mindset as a foundation for a towering success."

7. Sensory Language:
Incorporate sensory words for a more immersive experience:
"Picture yourself in a world where wealth flows like a crystal-clear river."
"Feel the excitement building as you step into a life of financial abundance."

8. Identity Statements:
Craft statements that reinforce your identity in relation to wealth:
"You are someone who effortlessly attracts opportunities for wealth."
"Being a wealth-conscious individual, your decisions lead to prosperity."

9. Future Pacing:
Guide your thoughts toward an envisioned future:
"Imagine yourself looking back at your journey, amazed by your wealth accomplishments."
"As you move forward, the path to wealth becomes clearer and more inviting."
10. Open-Ended Questions:
Pose questions that encourage expansive thinking:

"How can you leverage your strengths to create even greater wealth?"
"What exciting possibilities can unfold when you embrace a wealth-oriented mindset?"

Remember, these language patterns are designed to help you communicate with your subconscious mind more effectively. Consistently using these patterns can influence your beliefs and actions, aligning them with your wealth goals. However, while language patterns are powerful, they work best when combined with genuine intention and consistent action toward your desired outcomes.

1. The Tools of Advanced Language Patterns

1. Hypnotic language in advanced NLP is a way of communicating that engages the subconscious mind, making it more receptive to suggestions and ideas. It's not about putting someone into a literal trance but rather using language patterns that create a focused and suggestible state. When applied to enhancing your wealth mindset, hypnotic language can help you create a more receptive mental environment for positive beliefs about wealth. Here's how to use hypnotic language for wealth enhancement:

Use Positive Suggestions:
Frame your statements positively to encourage a shift in mindset. For example:
"You can begin to notice how your thoughts about wealth are becoming more positive."
"As you listen, you'll find yourself naturally attracted to ideas that promote financial abundance."

2. Utilize Power Words:
Incorporate words that evoke emotions and imagery related to wealth:
"Imagine the possibilities of wealth unfolding before you."
"Visualize yourself stepping confidently into a world of financial success."

3. Embed Commands:
Subtly include commands within your sentences to influence your subconscious mind:
"You may start to feel a growing sense of confidence in your ability to create wealth."
"Notice how you're naturally drawn to strategies that lead to financial prosperity."
4. Utilize Analogies and Stories:

Craft metaphors and stories that resonate with the subconscious mind:
"Just like a river flowing effortlessly, your wealth grows and expands."
"Think of your mind as a fertile soil, ready to cultivate the seeds of abundance."

5. Use Repetition:
Repeating key phrases can reinforce the desired mindset shift:
"With each word, you become more attuned to the idea of wealth."
"The more you hear these affirmations, the deeper they settle into your subconscious."

6. Slow and Calming Pace:
Speak in a measured, calm pace to create a soothing effect:
"Allow yourself to relax as you absorb these wealth-enhancing suggestions."
"As you listen, your mind unwinds and becomes open to new possibilities."

7. Speak Directly to the Listener:
Use "you" statements to personalize the experience:
"You are discovering that wealth creation is within your reach."
"As you integrate these thoughts, you're moving closer to your financial goals."

8. Engage the Senses:
Incorporate sensory language for a more immersive experience:
"Feel the excitement growing within you as you envision a life of abundance."
"Picture the vibrant colors of success filling your mind."

9. Create Vivid Imagery:
Paint a detailed picture in the listener's mind:

"Imagine yourself holding the keys to a vault of endless wealth possibilities."
"See yourself walking confidently along the path to financial prosperity."

10. Focus on Positive Outcomes:
Guide the listener's thoughts toward positive scenarios:
"Envision yourself reaping the rewards of your wealth-building efforts."
"As you listen, your mind opens to the endless potential of financial success."

Hypnotic language, when used responsibly and ethically, can help you communicate your wealth goals to your subconscious mind in a way that fosters belief and motivation. Remember that consistency and genuine intention play a significant role in the effectiveness of these language patterns.

Hypnotic language in advanced NLP involves using language patterns that create a state of focused attention and receptivity, similar to the state of hypnosis. These patterns are designed to bypass the critical conscious mind and communicate directly with the subconscious, making the listener more open to suggestion and influence. Here's an example of hypnotic language in an advanced NLP context:

Example: Elevating Your Wealth Mindset

"Close your eyes and take a deep, soothing breath. As you exhale, let go of any tension, allowing yourself to sink into a state of calm. Imagine yourself standing at the edge of a vast sea, with waves gently lapping at your feet. With each wave that touches you, feel a wave of relaxation washing over your entire being.
As you stand here, I want you to imagine a door in front of you. A door that leads to the realm of your subconscious mind, where your beliefs and perceptions reside. In a moment, I'm going to count from five down to one, and with each number, you'll feel this door opening, inviting you to explore the rich landscape of your inner thoughts.
Five... You can feel the door beginning to open, a warm light spilling out from within. Four... Your curiosity grows, as you step closer, drawn to the possibilities that await. Three... The light beckons you, inviting you to step through, to embark on a journey of transformation.
As you step through this doorway, you find yourself in a lush garden, vibrant and teeming with life. This garden is your subconscious mind, fertile ground for planting new beliefs and

nurturing empowering thoughts. Imagine that each thought you plant here is like a seed, and with each passing day, these seeds grow into mighty trees, their branches reaching toward the sky.

Now, imagine a stream running through this garden. This stream represents the flow of abundance in your life. It sparkles with opportunities and carries with it the energy of prosperity. See yourself stepping into the stream, feeling its cool waters enveloping you, cleansing you of any doubts or limitations.

And as you immerse yourself in this stream, listen closely to the whispers of your subconscious mind. Feel the gentle rhythm of your heartbeat syncing with the rhythm of the stream. Every beat, every ripple, reinforcing the truth that you are deserving of wealth, success, and boundless opportunities.

As you exit this garden, carrying with you the energy of abundance, remember that the power of your subconscious mind is always at your disposal. Whenever you encounter challenges, whenever you seek clarity, return to this garden, and watch as your beliefs bloom and thrive.

Now, in a moment, I'm going to count from one to five, and with each number, you'll return to full awareness, feeling refreshed, empowered, and aligned with your wealth mindset.

One... feeling a surge of energy returning to your body. Two... becoming aware of the sounds around you. Three... your mind clear and focused, ready to take on the world. Four... your eyes gently opening, bringing back the light of the present moment. And five... fully awake, fully present, and ready to embrace the abundance that is your birthright."

In this example, the language patterns used aim to induce a state of relaxation and openness while guiding the listener through a vivid visualization. The hypnotic language encourages the listener to tap into their subconscious mind and reprogram their beliefs about wealth and abundance.

2. Embedded Commands

Embedded commands are linguistic structures used in NLP to convey suggestions or commands within ordinary sentences. These commands are "embedded" within the sentence in a way that the subconscious mind picks up on them, even though they may not be overtly stated. When applied to enhancing your wealth mindset, embedded commands can help you direct your subconscious mind toward positive beliefs about wealth. Here's how to use embedded commands for wealth enhancement:

1. Choose a Command:
Decide on the command or suggestion you want to convey to your subconscious mind related to wealth, such as confidence, abundance, or positive actions.

2. Phrase Your Command:
Craft a sentence that includes the embedded command. The command is usually highlighted by altering its tonality, pace, or emphasis:
"As you explore the different ways to create wealth, you'll feel a growing sense of empowerment."

3. Match Your Command's Intensity:
Alter your voice subtly when delivering the embedded command. You might slightly raise or lower your tone, slow down or speed up your speech, or emphasize certain words.

4. Use Subtle Pauses:
Pause slightly before or after the embedded command to draw attention to it:
"You're discovering that your mindset can truly attract... wealth."
5. Overt and Covert Commands:
Combine overt and covert commands. An overt command is one that is obvious, while a covert command is subtly embedded:

"Notice how easily your mind embraces the idea of taking... decisive wealth-building actions."

6. Gesture to Reinforce:
Use a subtle gesture when delivering the command to reinforce the suggestion:
"As you envision your financial success, notice how your confidence rises *with your hand gently gesturing upward.*"

7. Repetition for Reinforcement:
Repeat the sentence with the embedded command to reinforce the suggestion:
"You have the ability to create wealth. You *have the ability* to create wealth."

8. Speak Confidently:
Deliver the sentence with confidence and conviction to reinforce the impact of the embedded command.

9. Tailor to Your Goal:
Ensure that the embedded command aligns with your specific wealth goal, whether it's confidence, wealth creation, or a positive mindset.

10. Contextual Integration:
Blend the sentence with the embedded command naturally into the conversation or your self-talk, so it flows seamlessly.

Example:
"As you take steps towards greater financial abundance, you'll begin to notice a new level of *confidence* growing within you."

Embedded commands can be a subtle yet powerful way to communicate with your subconscious mind and reinforce positive beliefs about wealth. Remember that the effectiveness of embedded commands relies on your consistency in using them and your genuine commitment to your wealth mindset goals.

Let's Understand it this way;

Embedded commands in advanced NLP involve subtly embedding a command within a sentence in a way that the conscious mind might not immediately recognize it, but the subconscious mind picks up on it. These commands are often given in a tone or context that makes them stand out from the rest of the sentence. Here's an example of embedded commands in an advanced NLP context:

Example: Igniting Your Wealth Potential

"As you listen to my words, you might begin to notice a growing sense of curiosity about your own potential. Perhaps you've already started to wonder how you can unlock the doors to your abundance, and that's perfectly natural. You see, the mind has a remarkable ability to discover new pathways of thinking, and it's almost as if you can imagine those pathways forming right now.

When you think about your goals, it's as if they're becoming clearer, as if your mind is drawing a vivid picture of your dreams. And as you contemplate these dreams, you may notice a subtle shift in your perspective, almost as if you're standing at a crossroads of possibilities. Each step you take, each decision you make, can lead you closer to the life you desire.

Imagine for a moment that you have a treasure map in your hands. A map that leads you to the treasure chest of your own potential. And just like a map, it's filled with directions and clues that guide you towards your goals. You might even sense a tingling excitement within you as you grasp the map tighter, ready to embark on this journey of discovery.

Now, here's the interesting part: your subconscious mind is absorbing these words, these ideas, and it's responding in ways you might not even consciously realize. Your subconscious mind is like a sponge, soaking up the suggestions and planting them deep within your thoughts.

And as you go about your day, you might catch yourself making decisions that align with your newfound perspective. Small choices that pave the way for greater abundance. It's as if your subconscious mind is nudging you, gently guiding you towards the actions that can lead to your own success.

So, go ahead and let your mind wander. Allow yourself to explore the depths of your potential, as if you're diving into a sea of endless opportunities. And as you do, you may find that these suggestions have already taken root within you, propelling you towards a future filled with prosperity."

In this example, the embedded commands are strategically woven into the narrative, guiding the listener's thoughts and subtly encouraging them to explore their potential and take empowered actions. While the embedded commands are not overtly obvious, they are designed to influence the subconscious mind and promote positive change in the listener's mindset.

Here are some examples of sentences with embedded commands:

"As you read this, you might notice your curiosity growing about the possibilities that lie ahead."

"Take a deep breath and relax, allowing yourself to feel more confident with every exhale."

"Picture yourself achieving your goals, and you'll find your motivation increasing naturally."

"Listen closely to the sound of my voice, and you'll discover a greater sense of calm washing over you."

"Consider the ways in which you can take inspired actions towards your dreams."

"Imagine stepping into a future where success is inevitable, and you'll feel a surge of determination."

"Pay attention to the subtle shifts in your thinking that lead you towards a more abundant mindset."

"Allow yourself to embrace new perspectives, and you'll find your creativity expanding effortlessly."

"Notice how your thoughts become clearer as you focus on the path that leads to your desired outcomes."

"As you reflect on your potential, you'll uncover hidden strengths that empower you to overcome challenges."

"Feel a wave of positivity washing over you as you consider the limitless opportunities that await."

"Picture yourself making choices that align with your goals, and watch your confidence soar."

"Notice the sensations in your body as you imagine stepping into a life of abundance."

"Explore the depths of your imagination and you'll unlock a wellspring of innovative ideas."

"Allow the words to sink in, and you'll discover a growing sense of belief in your own capabilities."

"Listen to the rhythm of your heartbeat, reminding you of the steady progress you're making."

"Imagine yourself taking bold steps forward, fueled by a sense of purpose and determination."

"As you absorb these suggestions, you'll find yourself naturally drawn to actions that lead to success."

"Consider how your mindset shapes your reality, and you'll see the potential for transformation."

"Feel a sense of empowerment building within you, encouraging you to seize every opportunity."

Remember, embedded commands work by subtly influencing the subconscious mind, so they are often integrated into the overall flow of a conversation or message. They can be especially effective when used in conjunction with appropriate tonality and pacing.

3. Presuppositions

Presuppositions are linguistic constructs used in advanced NLP that assume certain beliefs or ideas to be true, even if they aren't explicitly stated. These presuppositions can be leveraged to influence the way your mind processes information and to foster a more positive wealth mindset. Here's how to use presuppositions in advanced NLP for enhancing your relationship with wealth:

1. Present Wealth as a Given:
Frame statements that presuppose wealth as a natural outcome:
"As you continue on your journey, you'll find various ways to manifest financial success."
"The moment you embrace your potential for wealth, doors of opportunity begin to open."

2. Focus on Process, Not Possibility:
Assume that taking action toward wealth is a given, not a question:
"You may be curious about the effective strategies that lead to financial prosperity."
"Exploring the mindset of successful wealth creators becomes an exciting pursuit."

3. Direct Attention Positively:
Steer your focus toward positive aspects of wealth:
"You might be wondering how your mindset is contributing to your growing wealth."
"While some ponder obstacles, others are busy generating wealth."

4. Encourage a Shift in Perspective:
Assume a shift in thinking has already begun:
"You'll notice how your views about money evolve as you embrace your potential."
"Some realize the power of their mindset sooner than others, yet it's never too late to start."

5. Offer Multiple Options:
Present options while presupposing that progress is ongoing:
"Whether you choose to invest, innovate, or explore new avenues, your wealth journey continues."
"While learning from experts or experimenting with new strategies, your wealth path unfolds."

6. Imply an Existing Foundation:
Assume a foundation for wealth growth:
"Building on your existing knowledge, you'll see your financial prowess expand."
"Just as a foundation supports a strong structure, your current mindset supports wealth creation."

7. Highlight Gradual Transformation:
Imply that change is gradual and inevitable:
"Over time, you'll notice your wealth mindset naturally shifting toward abundance."
"As you experience various stages of growth, your financial reality changes."

8. Encourage Exploration:
Assume a curiosity and openness to new perspectives:
"While delving into the psychology of wealth, you'll uncover hidden potentials."
"Exploring different paths, you'll develop a comprehensive understanding of wealth."

9. Embed Presuppositions in Questions:
Frame questions that imply presuppositions:
"How does your perspective on wealth change when you consider all the opportunities available?"
"In what ways are you ready to harness your mindset for greater financial abundance?"

10. Consistency and Repetition:
Incorporate presuppositions consistently and repetitively to reinforce the desired mindset shift.

Using presuppositions can subtly shape your beliefs and attitudes about wealth by making certain assumptions a part of your mental framework. Consistent exposure to these presuppositions can help you adopt a more positive and empowered perspective on wealth.

Presuppositions are linguistic structures that assume the truth of certain statements or beliefs, often indirectly. They can be used in communication to guide someone's thinking or subtly introduce an idea.

Here are some examples of presuppositions related to wealth in the context of NLP:
"As you explore the various pathways to financial success, you'll discover exciting opportunities along the way."

> Presupposes that there are various pathways to financial success.

"Have you considered how investing wisely can lead to substantial returns?"

> Presupposes that investing wisely can lead to substantial returns.

"When you make decisions that align with your abundance mindset, your financial situation naturally improves."

> Presupposes the existence of an abundance mindset and the potential for financial improvement.

"Are you ready to unlock the potential of your wealth-building strategies?"

> Presupposes that the person has wealth-building strategies.

"Have you noticed how your beliefs about wealth influence your daily actions?"

Presupposes that beliefs about wealth influence actions.

"As you plan for your prosperous future, you'll find yourself taking steps toward achieving your financial goals."

Presupposes that the person is planning for a prosperous future and has financial goals.

"What steps will you take to maximize the benefits of your growing financial portfolio?"

Presupposes that the person has a growing financial portfolio and that there are benefits to maximize.

"When you adopt a mindset of abundance, you'll naturally attract wealth into your life."

Presupposes the possibility of adopting a mindset of abundance and attracting wealth.

"As you continue to educate yourself about financial strategies, you'll become more confident in your wealth-building abilities."

Presupposes the person is educating themselves about financial strategies and can become confident in wealth-building.

"Have you ever thought about the ways in which your financial decisions reflect your values?"

Presupposes that financial decisions reflect values.

"What insights have you gained from your previous successful financial endeavors?"

Presupposes that the person has gained insights from successful financial endeavors.

"When you focus on your goals with determination, you'll overcome any obstacles in your path to wealth."

> Presupposes that the person will focus on goals with determination and that obstacles can be overcome.

"Have you noticed the positive impact of your financial growth on other areas of your life?"

> Presupposes that there is a positive impact of financial growth on other life areas.

"As you reflect on your financial journey, you'll realize the power of your own resourcefulness."

> Presupposes that the person's financial journey involves resourcefulness.

"What strategies will you use to leverage your financial resources for greater success?"

> Presupposes that the person has financial resources and can leverage them for success.

These presuppositions can be used strategically to shape conversations and encourage a positive mindset related to wealth and abundance.

4. Time-Related Language

Time-related language in advanced NLP involves the strategic use of words and phrases related to time to influence how you perceive and approach wealth-related concepts. By incorporating time-related language, you can create a sense of progression, anticipation, and commitment to your wealth goals. Here's how to use time-related language in advanced NLP for enhancing your wealth mindset:

1. Future-Oriented Statements:
Frame your statements with a focus on future possibilities:
"In the coming months, your wealth-building efforts will yield remarkable results."
"As you move forward on your journey, financial abundance becomes increasingly tangible."

2. Time-Bound Commitment:
Incorporate specific time frames to emphasize commitment:
"Within the next year, you'll witness your financial situation transforming positively."
"By dedicating consistent effort, you'll see substantial wealth growth over the next few years."

3. Gradual Progression:
Highlight the gradual nature of wealth building:
"Over time, your financial mindset evolves, leading to sustained prosperity."
"As weeks turn into months, your wealth-building habits solidify and expand."

4. Seize the Moment:
Encourage taking action in the present while acknowledging time's passage:

"Now is the perfect moment to align your thoughts with wealth, ensuring a prosperous future."
"With every passing day, your decisions contribute to your financial success story."

5. Reflecting on Progress:
Suggest moments of reflection on your wealth journey:
"Looking back, you'll marvel at the strides you've made in your wealth mindset."
"Imagine the satisfaction of reviewing your achievements a year from **now."**

6. Continuous Transformation:
Use language that implies ongoing change and evolution:
"As you continue to explore wealth-building strategies, your mindset undergoes positive shifts."
"Your perception of wealth adapts as you experience new opportunities."

7. Anchoring Success in Time:
Tie your affirmations to specific moments in time:
"By this time next year, you'll be reaping the rewards of your wealth-focused actions."
"Imagine celebrating the anniversary of your commitment to wealth, celebrating your growth."

8. Creating a Timeline:
Visualize your journey with a temporal timeline:
"Picture a timeline stretching ahead, marked by achievements and wealth milestones."
"Place each success and insight on your timeline, showcasing your advancement."

9. Reminding of Upcoming Opportunities:
Prompt awareness of upcoming opportunities:

"As the year progresses, you'll find various avenues to expand your wealth portfolio."
"With each season, new financial possibilities emerge, ready for your exploration."

10. Setting Future Goals:
Frame your goals within a specific timeframe:
"Within the next five years, you'll have achieved your vision of financial independence."

"By the end of this decade, your wealth mindset will be a cornerstone of your success."
By incorporating time-related language, you shape your perspective on wealth by framing it within a timeline of progress and evolution. This can foster a sense of commitment, anticipation, and proactive action toward your wealth goals.

Here are some examples of sentences using time-related language in the context of NLP for wealth:

"Imagine yourself looking back a year from now, proud of the financial progress you've made."

"As you take consistent actions towards your wealth goals, you'll notice positive changes within weeks."

"By setting clear financial targets and working diligently, you'll realize your vision of success sooner than you think."
"Picture yourself a few months from today, enjoying the rewards of your disciplined financial choices."

"As you continue to invest wisely, you'll see your wealth growing steadily over the course of the next year."

"Consider how your commitment to learning about smart investments will pay off in the coming months."

"When you start implementing effective budgeting strategies today, you'll experience greater financial freedom in the near future."

"By consistently saving a portion of your income, you'll create a substantial nest egg over the next few years."

"As the seasons change, so will your financial situation when you embrace the power of compound interest."

"Think about the impact of making small adjustments to your financial habits; you'll see significant improvements over time."
"Imagine yourself attending that dream vacation next year, made possible by the wealth-building decisions you're making today."

"By setting short-term milestones, you'll ensure that you're progressing steadily towards your long-term wealth aspirations."

"When you dedicate just a few minutes daily to reviewing your financial plans, you'll keep yourself on track for success."

"As you look ahead to your retirement years, envision the peace of mind that comes from a well-prepared financial strategy."

"Consider the satisfaction of achieving your wealth goals, knowing that your consistent efforts have paid off in record time."

Using time-related language can help anchor the idea of progress and success in the listener's mind while encouraging them to take action towards their wealth-related objectives.

5. The Cause-and-Effect

The cause-and-effect language pattern in advanced NLP involves establishing a relationship between actions (cause) and their outcomes (effect). By using this pattern strategically, you can influence your mindset and behaviors related to wealth. Here's how to use the cause-and-effect language pattern in advanced NLP to enhance your wealth mindset:

1. Highlight Positive Actions:
Connect positive actions with favorable outcomes:
"By consistently saving a portion of your income, you create a pathway to financial security."
"When you invest time in learning about wealth strategies, your confidence in financial decision-making grows."

2. Emphasize Mindset Shifts:

Link mindset shifts to tangible results:
"As your beliefs about wealth become more empowering, your financial decisions naturally align with success."
"When you adopt a proactive wealth mindset, you attract opportunities that accelerate your financial growth."

3. Reinforce Positive Habits:
Connect habits to their long-term effects:
"Each day you dedicate to expanding your knowledge of wealth accumulates into a wealth of wisdom."
"When you commit to consistent action, the compound effect ensures your wealth journey gains momentum."

4. Motivate Taking Initiative:
Highlight the empowering effects of taking initiative:
"By taking the initiative to explore new income streams, you're setting the stage for greater financial abundance."

"As you initiate conversations about financial opportunities, you open doors to partnerships that propel your wealth journey."

5. Inspire Accountability:
Link accountability to desired outcomes:
"When you hold yourself accountable for your financial decisions, you direct your path toward prosperity."
"By embracing financial responsibility, you cultivate an environment conducive to wealth creation."

6. Connect Learning and Growth:
Tie learning to personal growth and success:
"Every book you read, every course you take, contributes to your growth as a wealth-conscious individual."
"As you commit to continuous learning, you're planting seeds of knowledge that will yield a bountiful harvest of wealth."

7. Harness Visualization:
Visualize the effect of your actions on your wealth journey:
"Imagine each positive choice you make as a stepping stone on the path to financial success."
"See your commitment to wealth-building as a torch that lights up the way to your prosperous future."

8. Emphasize Long-Term Vision:
Connect present actions with your long-term vision:
"By making strategic investments now, you're building a bridge to the future of financial freedom."
"When you prioritize building your wealth toolkit, you're equipping yourself for a lifetime of prosperity."

9. Link Courage and Reward:
Associate stepping out of your comfort zone with rewarding outcomes:

"As you gather the courage to explore unconventional opportunities, you pave the way for extraordinary wealth."
"When you embrace risk intelligently, you set the stage for exceptional rewards in your financial journey."

10. Foster Momentum:
Showcase the compounding effect of consistent effort:
"Each positive action adds a drop to your reservoir of wealth, gradually filling it to overflowing."
"With every decision rooted in abundance, you create a momentum that propels you toward financial greatness."
Using the cause-and-effect language pattern can help you internalize the connection between your actions and their impact on your wealth journey. This pattern encourages proactive behaviors and mindset shifts that align with your financial aspirations.

Here are some examples of sentences using cause-and-effect language in the context of NLP for wealth:

"When you consistently invest your time in learning about financial strategies, you'll naturally see an increase in your wealth over time."

"By making informed decisions about your investments, you'll create a ripple effect that leads to financial prosperity."

"As you take steps to diversify your income streams, you'll discover a direct correlation between your efforts and your growing wealth."

"When you prioritize saving a portion of your earnings, you're setting in motion a chain reaction that will provide financial security down the line."

"The more you align your actions with your financial goals, the more you'll witness the cause-and-effect relationship between intention and achievement."

"As you consistently apply your financial knowledge, you'll observe a direct link between your efforts and the steady growth of your wealth."

"When you leverage your skills and talents to create value for others, you'll initiate a series of events that lead to both personal fulfillment and financial gain."

"By cultivating a mindset of abundance, you're initiating a shift in your beliefs that will naturally attract more opportunities for wealth."

"As you actively seek out mentors and role models, you're initiating a process of accelerated learning that will undoubtedly impact your financial success."

"The more you take calculated risks and step out of your comfort zone, the more you'll realize the effect this courage has on your ability to create wealth."

"When you invest time in building meaningful relationships, you'll find that these connections can have a direct impact on your wealth-building journey."

"As you consistently apply the principles of responsible financial management, you'll recognize the cause-and-effect relationship between your actions and your financial stability."

"The choices you make today, whether large or small, have a direct effect on the trajectory of your financial future."

"By setting clear goals and breaking them down into actionable steps, you're creating a roadmap for wealth that leads to a series of achievements."

"When you embrace a growth-oriented mindset and commit to continuous self-improvement, you'll see a direct correlation between personal development and financial growth."

Using cause-and-effect language can help emphasize the direct relationship between actions, choices, and their impact on wealth-building outcomes.

6. Analogical Framing

Analogical framing in NLP involves using analogies or metaphors to explain complex concepts or ideas by comparing them to something more relatable. When applied to enhancing your wealth mindset, analogical framing can help you understand wealth-related concepts in a more relatable and tangible way. Here's how to use analogical framing in advanced NLP for enhancing your relationship with wealth:

1. Financial Garden:
Imagine your wealth journey as tending to a garden. Just as a gardener nurtures plants with care, you nurture your financial endeavors with diligence, watching them grow and flourish over time.

2. Wealth as a Puzzle:
Consider your financial life as a puzzle. Each piece represents a decision or action that, when fitted together strategically, reveals the bigger picture of your wealth success.

3. Wealth Blueprint:
Visualize your financial path as a blueprint. Just as architects plan and build structures, you're designing and constructing a solid foundation for your wealth future.

4. Wealth as a Journey:
Think of wealth creation as embarking on a journey. Your actions and choices become steps along the path, leading you to discover new horizons of prosperity.

5. Financial Seeds:
Envision your actions as planting seeds of wealth. Like a gardener, you sow the seeds of your efforts, nurturing them to grow into bountiful financial rewards.

6. Wealth Mindset as a Compass:
Imagine your wealth mindset as a compass guiding your decisions. Just as a compass ensures you stay on course during a journey, your mindset directs you toward financial success.

7. Financial Reservoir:
Think of your wealth-building efforts as filling a reservoir drop by drop. Each action contributes to the steady accumulation of wealth, eventually overflowing with abundance.

8. Wealth Well:
Picture your wealth journey as drawing from a well of opportunities. Like drawing water from a well, your efforts yield the nourishment of financial growth.

9. Financial Puzzle Pieces:
Compare your financial knowledge to puzzle pieces. Just as each piece contributes to the puzzle's completion, each piece of financial knowledge contributes to your wealth success.

10. Wealth as a Garden of Opportunities:
Envision your financial landscape as a garden of opportunities. Just as a garden offers an array of plants to cultivate, your financial world offers various ways to nurture wealth.

Using analogical framing can make abstract wealth concepts more concrete and relatable. It aids in understanding and internalizing these ideas, making them more accessible and actionable in your wealth-building journey.

Analogical framing in NLP involves drawing parallels between different situations or concepts to convey a particular message or understanding. Here are some examples of sentences using analogical framing in the context of NLP for wealth:

"Think of your financial journey as a marathon. Just as each step taken with determination brings you closer to the finish line, every financial decision you make propels you towards your wealth goals."

"Much like tending to a garden, nurturing your investments requires patience and attention. As you sow the seeds of wise choices, you'll eventually reap a bountiful harvest of financial rewards."

"Consider your wealth-building strategy as a puzzle. Each financial move you make is like placing a piece in the puzzle, gradually revealing the bigger picture of your prosperity."

"Just as a skilled conductor orchestrates a symphony, you have the power to harmonize your financial elements. Balancing income, expenses, and investments creates a beautiful financial melody."

"Imagine your financial goals as destinations on a map. Every smart decision is a step closer to reaching these destinations, guiding you through the journey of wealth creation."

"Think of your wealth mindset as a muscle. The more you exercise it through positive thinking and constructive actions, the stronger and more resilient it becomes."

"Picture your financial growth as a tree. With strong roots in education and sound decisions, it grows tall and bears the fruit of financial success."

"Much like building a sturdy house, your wealth foundation requires careful planning and solid principles. As you lay each brick of knowledge, your financial structure becomes unshakable."

"Consider your wealth-building journey as an artist's canvas. Every stroke of financial wisdom and every vibrant decision adds depth and richness to the masterpiece of your life."

"Imagine your financial path as a river. It may encounter obstacles, but as you navigate with purpose, you'll find alternative routes and create your own channels of abundance."

"Think of your mind as a garden of thoughts. Just as you weed out negativity and nurture positivity, you cultivate the fertile ground for a bountiful harvest of wealth."

"Much like a captain navigating a ship through uncharted waters, you guide your financial vessel towards unexplored territories of success, using your knowledge as a compass."

"Imagine your financial goals as constellations in the sky. Each decision you make adds another star, illuminating the path that leads to your desired financial constellation."

"Think of your financial plan as a recipe. By carefully measuring your resources and mixing in strategic actions, you create a dish of wealth that satisfies your aspirations."

"Consider your wealth journey as a mountain climb. As you ascend towards your goals, you gain a new perspective with every step, appreciating the challenges that lead to triumph."

Analogical framing allows you to connect complex concepts with familiar imagery, making it easier for individuals to grasp and relate to the ideas being presented.

7. Identity Statements

Identity statements in NLP involve shaping your self-concept and beliefs about who you are. When applied to enhancing your wealth mindset, identity statements can help you develop a stronger sense of identity aligned with wealth creation. Here's how to use identity statements in advanced NLP for enhancing your relationship with wealth:

1. I Am a Wealth Creator:
Affirm your identity as someone who creates wealth through your actions and decisions:
"I am a wealth creator, constantly seeking opportunities to grow my financial resources."
"I am a skilled navigator of the wealth landscape, charting my course toward abundance."

2. I Embrace Prosperity:
Declare your openness to embrace prosperity in all its forms:
"I am open to receiving wealth and abundance in every aspect of my life."
"I am a magnet for financial success, attracting prosperity effortlessly."

3. I Am a Financial Visionary:
Define yourself as a visionary who sees possibilities beyond the present:
"I am a financial visionary, envisioning paths to wealth where others see limitations."
"I possess the foresight to recognize and seize opportunities that lead to financial greatness."

4. I Make Empowered Financial Decisions:
Assert your ability to make confident and empowered financial choices:
"I make decisions that align with my wealth goals, ensuring a secure financial future."
"I am a shrewd decision-maker, steering my finances toward success."

5. I Am Aligned with Abundance:
Confirm your alignment with the energy of abundance:
"I am in perfect harmony with the flow of abundance, attracting wealth effortlessly."
"My thoughts and actions are in sync with the rhythm of prosperity."

6. I Am the Author of My Financial Story:
Recognize your role in shaping your financial narrative:
"I am the author of my financial story, scripting a tale of wealth and achievement."
"I possess the power to rewrite my financial script, crafting a tale of boundless abundance."

7. I Am a Wealth Magnet:
Portray yourself as a magnet for wealth and opportunities:
"I am a magnet for financial blessings, drawing wealth toward me from all directions."
"My presence attracts opportunities that lead to financial enrichment."

8. I Embrace Wealth-Building Habits:
Acknowledge your commitment to nurturing wealth-building habits:
"I am dedicated to cultivating habits that propel me toward financial success."

"I embrace daily practices that reinforce my wealth-conscious mindset."

9. I Am Worthy of Financial Prosperity:
Recognize your inherent worthiness to experience financial prosperity:
"I am worthy of enjoying financial abundance and all the opportunities it brings."
"I deserve to live a life of financial fulfillment and freedom."

10. I Am a Steward of Wealth:
Affirm your responsibility in managing and growing your wealth:
"I am a responsible steward of my financial resources, nurturing them for future growth."
"I take pride in managing my wealth wisely and ethically."

Using identity statements can help shape your self-concept and beliefs, aligning them with a wealth-conscious mindset. By consistently affirming these statements, you reinforce your commitment to wealth creation and cultivate a stronger relationship with financial success.

8. Open-Ended Questions

Open-ended questions in advanced NLP are designed to encourage deeper thinking, exploration, and introspection. When applied to enhancing your wealth mindset, open-ended questions can prompt you to examine your beliefs, perspectives, and actions related to wealth in a more profound way. Here's how to use open-ended questions in advanced NLP for enhancing your relationship with wealth:

1. "What Does Wealth Mean to Me?"
Encourage self-reflection on your personal definition of wealth and its significance in your life.

2. "How Can I Expand My Wealth Consciousness?"
Prompt exploration of ways to broaden your awareness and understanding of wealth.

3. "What Limiting Beliefs Am I Ready to Release?"
Invite introspection on any negative beliefs that may be holding you back from financial success.

4. "What Positive Actions Can I Take Today to Move Closer to My Wealth Goals?"
Stimulate proactive thinking about practical steps you can take to advance your wealth journey.

5. "In What Ways Can I Leverage My Strengths to Create Wealth?"
Encourage identification of your unique skills and talents that can contribute to your financial growth.

6. "What Habits Align with a Wealthy Mindset?"
Prompt exploration of daily habits that support a mindset conducive to wealth creation.

7. "How Can I Embrace Risk Wisely to Propel My Financial Growth?"
Encourage contemplation on how calculated risks can lead to greater opportunities for wealth.

8. "What Can I Learn from Past Financial Experiences?"
Invite reflection on the lessons and insights gained from previous financial situations.

9. "How Does My Attitude Towards Money Impact My Wealth Journey?"
Stimulate self-awareness about the role your attitude plays in your relationship with money and wealth.

10. "What Legacy of Financial Success Do I Want to Leave Behind?"
Encourage consideration of the long-term impact of your financial decisions and actions.

11. "What Strategies Can I Implement to Diversify My Income Sources?"
Prompt exploration of ways to create multiple streams of income for enhanced financial security.

12. "How Can I Cultivate a Sense of Gratitude for My Current Financial Situation?"
Encourage a shift in perspective towards appreciating your present financial circumstances.

13. "What Inspirational Role Models Can I Learn from in the Field of Wealth?"
Stimulate research and introspection on individuals who have achieved financial success and can serve as mentors.

14. "How Can I Balance Present Enjoyment with Future Financial Security?"
Encourage consideration of the balance between enjoying the present and planning for the future.

15. "What Vision of Wealth Do I Want to Manifest in My Life?"
Prompt visualization and clarification of your ultimate vision for wealth and its manifestation.

Using open-ended questions allows you to explore your wealth mindset from various angles, gaining deeper insights and fostering a more comprehensive understanding of your relationship with wealth. This reflective process can lead to meaningful shifts in your mindset and behaviors related to financial success.

Here are more examples of open-ended questions in the context of NLP for exploring wealth-related thoughts and possibilities:

"What does financial abundance mean to you personally?"

"How do you envision your ideal financial future?"

"In what ways can you leverage your skills to create new income streams?"

"What steps are you taking to enhance your financial knowledge?"

"What strategies are you considering to diversify your investment portfolio?"

"How do you plan to balance your short-term financial goals with your long-term aspirations?"

"What opportunities do you see in the current market trends for wealth creation?"

"What actions can you take to align your spending habits with your financial goals?"

"How will achieving your wealth goals positively impact other areas of your life?"

"What role does self-discipline play in your pursuit of financial success?"

"What are some innovative ways you can add value to your career or business?"

"How can you cultivate a mindset of abundance and attract more wealth into your life?"

"What resources or skills do you possess that can contribute to your financial growth?"

"What strategies do you have in place to overcome any potential financial challenges?"

"How will your current financial decisions shape the legacy you leave behind?"

"What motivates you to consistently take steps towards achieving your financial goals?"

"How do you see your financial journey evolving over the next few years?"

"What impact can networking and building connections have on your wealth-building journey?"

"What habits or behaviors might be holding you back from reaching your full financial potential?"
"How can you create a balance between enjoying your wealth and responsibly managing it?"

Open-ended questions encourage deeper reflection, exploration, and dialogue about wealth-related topics, allowing individuals to express their thoughts and aspirations freely.

Gratitude

Gratitude is like giving a big thank you to life. It's not exactly a magic trick, but it can make you feel really good. Here's how you can do it using some brain tricks called NLP (Neuro-Linguistic Programming).

First, decide that you want to be more grateful. Think of it as making a promise to yourself.

Next, find a special way to show gratitude. It could be a small thing, like touching your heart or tapping your fingers together. This is your secret sign for gratitude.

Every day, take a few minutes to think about the good stuff in your life. Maybe it's your family, a fun day, or even just having a cozy bed. While you think about these things, do your secret gratitude sign. It's like a secret code that tells your brain, "Hey, we're feeling thankful right now!"

You can also use nice words when you talk to yourself. Tell yourself things like, "I'm really lucky to have so many good things in my life," or "When I'm grateful, good things come my way."

Sometimes, imagine all the good things like a movie in your mind. See them, feel them, and enjoy them in your imagination. It's like having your own happy movie theater inside your head.

If you catch yourself thinking something not-so-nice, like "I don't like this" or "I'm not happy," try to change it. Think about something you're thankful for instead.

You can also write down all the things you're grateful for in a special journal. It's like keeping a treasure chest of good feelings.

Lastly, don't forget to say thank you to the people who make your life better. A simple thank-you can make their day brighter too.

So, by using these tricks from NLP and practicing gratitude, you can make your heart feel warmer, your mind feel lighter, and your days feel happier. It's like a little bit of magic you create for yourself every day.

Practicing gratitude can indeed improve your emotional and mental "vibration" or state of being. Gratitude is like a positive energy that radiates from you when you focus on the things you're thankful for. Here's how it works:
Raises Positivity: Gratitude shifts your focus from what's lacking or negative in your life to what's abundant and positive. This change in perspective naturally lifts your mood and makes you feel more positive.

Reduces Stress: When you're grateful, your brain releases "feel-good" chemicals like dopamine and serotonin. This helps reduce stress and anxiety, making you feel calmer and more at ease.

Enhances Relationships: Expressing gratitude towards others strengthens your relationships. It fosters a sense of connection and appreciation, leading to better interactions and deeper bonds.

Attracts Positivity: Like attracts like. When you emit positive vibes through gratitude, you tend to attract more positive experiences and people into your life.

Improves Mental Health: Regular gratitude practice has been linked to improved mental health. It can reduce symptoms of depression and increase overall life satisfaction.

Boosts Resilience: Grateful people often cope better with challenges and setbacks. They have a more resilient mindset, which helps them bounce back from difficulties.

Promotes Physical Health: Gratitude isn't just good for your mind; it's good for your body too. It's associated with better sleep, a stronger immune system, and lower blood pressure.

So, when you practice gratitude, you're essentially raising your emotional and mental frequency to a more positive and harmonious level. This positive "vibration" can have a ripple effect on your life, leading to increased happiness, improved relationships, and even better health.

By understanding the concept of neuroplasticity and utilizing techniques like Neuro-Linguistic Programming (NLP), individuals can effectively change their neural wiring and thought patterns related to money and wealth.
NLP provides a structured framework to reshape negative beliefs, attitudes, and behaviors and replace them with positive, empowering ones.

Through consistent practice of NLP techniques, individuals can reprogram their subconscious mind to align with their financial goals and aspirations. Visualization, positive affirmations, language patterns, and other NLP tools work to create new neural pathways that support a mindset of abundance, wealth creation, and success.

However, it's important to emphasize that while NLP and neural rewiring can be powerful tools, they are most effective when combined with practical actions, financial literacy, and a holistic approach to wealth-building.

Cultivating a balanced mindset, making informed decisions, and taking proactive steps towards financial success are all essential components of a comprehensive strategy for achieving money goals and building lasting wealth.

In the journey through this book on utilizing Neuro-Linguistic Programming (NLP) techniques for wealth creation, we've uncovered the extraordinary potential of our brains to shape our financial destinies. These techniques, rooted in the science of the mind and language, have provided us with a roadmap to rewire our neural pathways for prosperity.

As we conclude this voyage, remember that true wealth isn't just about money; it's about the freedom, opportunities, and security that financial abundance can bring. NLP empowers us to break free from limiting beliefs, develop a prosperous mindset, and attract wealth with intention and clarity.

So, as you embark on your path to financial abundance, carry these NLP tools in your arsenal with confidence. Your brain is a powerful tool waiting to be programmed for success. Through the techniques explored in this book, you have the ability to rewrite your financial story, create lasting wealth, and live a life of purpose and fulfilment. The journey to wealth begins with the transformation of your thoughts, and NLP is your key to unlocking that transformation.
May your financial dreams become a reality, and may you find not only wealth but also true abundance in every aspect of your life.

The Miracle Books

About the Author

Prof. Abha Bhardwaj Sharma, an esteemed English professor and the visionary force behind the Miracle English Language & Literature Institute since 1998, has flourished for over 25 impactful years in the realm of education. Her journey extends beyond the traditional boundaries of academia, as she is also an accomplished NLP (Neuro-Linguistic Programming) coach and practitioner. Prof. Abha's multifaceted expertise shines through her eloquent narratives, reflecting her profound grasp of English literature, linguistic structures, and the transformative power of NLP.

Her literary works are more than just written words; they are explorations through the rich corridors of literature, painted with vivid imagery and laced with thought-provoking insights. As an NLP coach, Prof. Abha has penned several influential books, offering tools and techniques that empower individuals to rewrite their life stories, overcome personal challenges, and unlock their full potential.

In her role as a mentor, Prof. Abha has shaped the minds of countless scholars, instilling in them a deep appreciation for the nuances of the English language & Literature. Her guidance in linguistics and literature, combined with her expertise in NLP, makes her a unique beacon of knowledge and inspiration. Her profound influence on English Language Literature and Linguistics Education, coupled with her contributions to the field of personal development through NLP, has left an indelible mark on academia and beyond.

Prof. Abha Bhardwaj Sharma's legacy as an author, educator, and NLP coach continues to inspire, educate, and transform lives, making her a distinguished figure in the intersection of language, literature, and personal growth.

www.ingramcontent.com/pod-product-compliance
Lightning Source LLC
LaVergne TN
LVHW021139160826
845679LV00023B/1976

* 9 7 9 8 8 9 2 7 7 0 9 8 9 *